Small Business Barriers and Battlefields

Adding Reality to the American Dream

by
Robert Fleury

Copyright 1994 by Robert E. Fleury

All rights reserved. No part of this book may be reproduced in any form or by any electronic or mechanical means including information storage and retrieval systems--except in the case of brief quotations embodied in critical articles or reviews--without permission in writing from it's publisher, Matahari Publishing.

Matahari Publishing
36W794 Stonebridge
St. Charles, Illinois USA
60175
(708) 584-7426
Fax (708) 584-7426

Editorial: Paul Halvey, CustomDesign Communications, North Riverside, IL
Design and Production: Paul Halvey, CustomDesign Communications
Proofreading and Cover Design: Rita Fleury

This publication is designed to provide an individual perspective in regard to the subject matter covered. It is sold with the understanding that neither the publisher nor author are engaged in rendering professional service or advice. If such advice or service is needed, a competent professional person should be retained.

Library Of Congress Cataloging-in-Publication Data

Fleury, Robert E. (Robert Earl), 1941-
   Small business barriers and battlefields: adding reality to the american dream / by Robert E. Fleury.

Library of Congress Catalogue Card Number: 94-79569

   Includes index
   ISBN 0-9642814-0-6 : hardcover -- ISBN 0-9642814-1-4 : paperback

---

Printed and bound in the United States of America
10 9 8 7 6 5 4 3 2 1

658.022
F618

ACKNOWLEDGMENT

Contributions to this book have come from many small businesses I have worked with over the years. Particularly, it is subscribers to my newsletter, *The Smalltime Entrepreneur*, who have provided the impetus for this work. It is the regimentation required to generate tri-weekly fresh small business material that has given this book its form. Their subscriptions have helped fund a book that otherwise would not likely have been written. My daughter, Rita, has designed the book cover and made editorial contributions. Mr. Paul Halvey has made a professional contribution in pulling the material into a book. These combined contributions are greatly appreciated and are hereby acknowledged.

DEDICATION

This book is dedicated to two groups of entrepreneurs--to those whose sleepless nights, stressful days, empty bank accounts and even untimely demises have left behind valuable lessons, and to those with the understanding and good fortune to benefit from those hard-earned insights.

Table of Contents

Introduction		i
Part One	The First Barrier--Focus	1
Chapter :	1. Market Research	3
	2. Reading the Economic Landscape	11
	3. The Alternative to Borrowing	17
Part Two	The Information Barrier	23
Chapter:	4. Deciding When to Computerize	25
	5. The Threshold Business Computer System	31
	6. The Printer	37
Part Three	The Battle to Manage Resources	41
Chapter:	7. Money Management	43
	8. Accounting	49
	9. Pricing Policies	57
	10. Managing Cash for Taxes	63
	11. Cost Cutting	71
Part Four	Battles of the Mind	77
Chapter:	12. Physical and Mental Addictions in Business	79
	Part One...Substance Addiction	80
	Part Two...Process Addiction	88
	13. The Behaviors of Process Addictions	91
	14. Doing Business With the Process Addict	99
Part Five	Barriers of Thought	107
Chapter:	15. The Infrastructure of Decision Making	109
	16. The Competitive Edge in a Pricing Strategy	115
	17. The Logic of Business	121
	18. Sex and the Small Business	127
Part Six	The Documentation Barrier	135
Chapter:	19. The Courtroom Battle and the Small Business	137
	20. Keeping Records	147
Part Seven	The Battle for Growth	153

Chapter:	21. Promoting the Small Business	155
	22. The Sales Portfolio	159
	23. Sales--The Follow Up	163
	24. The Hidden Cost of Hiring	169
	25. The Battle of Image vs. Ego	175
	26. The Entrepreneurial Mirage	181

Conclusion		187
Index		191
Ordering Information		193

Illustrations

Figure One	The Prime Rate Curve	12
Figure Two	Income Statement	53
Figure Three	The Quick Cash Report	54
Figure Four	IRS Form 2210, side one	66
Figure Five	IRS Form 2210, side two	67

INTRODUCTION

The inspiration for this book came from the unexpected results of my first book, *"The Small Business Survival Guide."* My premise was that most business failure stemmed from the inability of entrepreneurs to use accounting principles to gather the information that is crucial to making correct business decisions. I argued that because most businesses are profitable when they go under, clearly, earlier decisions set the company on a financial course that was doomed to fail. *"The Small Business Survival Guide"* identified a series of reasonable and logical financial tenets by which the survival rate of small business could be dramatically improved. Those concepts took the physical form of the *No Entry Accounting*™ system, a sort box using common sense names to group business documents in such a way as to quickly and easily provide key financial and tax information.

"The Small Business Survival Guide" and its insights into the unwillingness of most entrepreneurs to get close to their accounting drew rave reviews from entrepreneurs, students, and the media in North America and Europe. Yet after many seminars and classes, and delivering small business computer systems based on *No Entry Accounting*™, few businesses benefited as dramatically as I had hoped.

Barriers and Battlefields

In my search to learn why, I discovered another hidden truth about entrepreneurs--a flaw that in many cases is fatal to their business. That is, without realizing it, entrepreneurs make most of their business decisions based on a multitude of influences other than logic. That is why so many entrepreneurs loath accounting--it brings a mathematical logic to the running of an enterprise. Such cold, clear reasoning runs counter to the inner workings of their own minds.

"Small Business Barriers and Battlefields" is for those entrepreneurs who need help reaching the level at which logic is the guiding force behind their decisions and the operation of their business. You do not have to be logical in the way mathematics is logical. There is plenty of room in small business for personality. But you must learn to recognize when forces other than logic are driving your personality and are behind your behavior and decisions. Then you need to connect this new insight to your business decisions so that you do not choose a path that leads to failure.

Acknowledging that most small business activity is illogical has benefited me considerably in my own business. It has helped me to deal with very difficult customers, whose demands in the past would have left me reeling in anger or feeling that I had been hustled. It has given me insight into vendors and identified those who deserve my business, those to whom I even owe a debt of gratitude, and those with whom I will never spend another dime. It has helped me to deal with employees whose way of thinking makes no logical connection between a paycheck and the need to perform useful, productive labor. Most importantly, it has shown me how I have tripped up myself as often as others have done it to me.

I have learned that we can be our own worst enemy. As entrepreneurs, everything we do in operating our business ultimately has a direct impact upon the cash we have for running our enterprise. Since cash is the life blood of any financial enterprise, we must gain a logical control of all the forces which may impact that life blood--particularly when that force is ourselves.

I have found no literature that explores this concept, let alone offers a solution. But over the years, I have seen many entrepreneurs battle what they thought were market forces, but turned out to be their own demons. Every case study in this book comes from my firsthand experiences with entrepreneurs in a variety of fields. And I have included my personal experiences building my *No Entry*

Accounting business from the flash of an idea to a product with sales from North America to England. Join me as we explore the barriers and battlefields that each entrepreneur must cross in pursuit of the American dream.

PART ONE

THE FIRST BARRIER--FOCUS

Chapter One

MARKET RESEARCH

Whether you are just beginning to look for a way into the entrepreneurial arena or your fight for self employment is in full swing, the basic principles of market research have value. Market research provides the crucial first ingredient in the recipe for any business--focus. Research can provide inspiration for those who have not settled on a specific product or business. It can provide direction to those exploring a new, unfamiliar business or those expanding into some new area associated with an existing business. Research can help devise a plan of attack for those with a product or service who are looking for the best method to bring it to market.

I regularly turn to the principles of market research in my business ventures. My own product, *The No Entry Accounting System*™, illustrates some of the many steps involved and offers insight into the nature of understanding the market and refining the product in response to consumers. Market research techniques helped me turn a gut feeling into a computer software product for business. It's a long march between hunch and product. But market research kept me on a course in which the natural progression was clear. Best of all, I got the job done with no cash outlay. Most market research costs only your time.

Throughout this book, case histories will be used to illustrate business concepts. Each case study comes from my direct contact with entrepreneurs in various fields. Let us begin with my firsthand experiences building my *No Entry Accounting* business. It is a lengthy case study, but it illustrates several key points along the path of market research. By covering it first, we can refer back to this story when we turn to other small business concepts.

Defining the Problem

After years of cold calling on small businesses selling business computer products, I believed that I had a good feel for the marketplace. Firsthand experience convinced me that small business owners were surprisingly afraid of doing their own accounting, and worked hard to avoid it. Yet I was certain, through operating various businesses myself over the years, that it was crucial for small business owners to deal personally with accounting if they were to succeed. Such a conclusion represents a significant piece of research in itself. It is the first step in a market research project--identify a specific need. Through personal observation and firsthand experience, I had researched a marketplace and discovered a compelling, unfilled need.

The Problem

Recognizing a specific need is fundamental to creating a new product or service because researchers know that 90 percent of the solution is properly defining the problem. I defined the problem this way:

> *"Small business people fear or loath the process they need most--keeping track of business transactions."*

The problem could be more clearly defined by listing contributing factors which permitted the main problem to exist.

Sub Problems

1. *Recordkeeping, particularly accounting, is perceived as complicated by small business people.*
2. *Available solutions do not serve the small business person.*

a. *Accounting fees require too large a percentage of a small business' revenue.*
   b. *College classes take too much of the entrepreneur's time.*

I believed that the problem and sub problems contributed to the high failure rate of small businesses. If accounting were easier, many more businesses would succeed.

How the Problem is Perceived

The first barrier to clear, then, was the perception by small business owners that accounting is too difficult for them to master. This view is the result of a deliberate effort to make teaching and performing conventional accounting tasks more complicated than necessary. The result is a steady supply of clients for accountants fluent in a language of their own creation, that in many cases has nothing particularly useful to say to the small business person. The problem created a need for a system that was much simpler than conventional accounting by which people could learn valuable cash management principles that would keep them in business.

Testing Alternatives

From my experience with small business computers, I knew they were too expensive for 95 percent of the businesses I was targeting. Accountants were also too costly. Library research of corporate income statements showed that accounting totals less than 1 percent of revenue. Yet I had seen small businesses pay as much as 35 percent.

I tried to do what my target customer would attempt--accounting the conventional way, with ledgers, journals and such. It took too much time and even after several semesters of accounting, I didn't feel certain I was getting it right. Ignoring the problem until tax time and sorting a year's worth of paperwork on the living room floor proved definitely not the way to go. It took days to find everything, sort the piles and complete the proper tax forms. Business--and revenue flow--came to a standstill. All this only to find I had missed three quarterly tax deposits and now owed penalties and late charges. Next, I tried file folders, which proved impractical when seeking data on the current month and year-to-date problems. It was also impractical for document handling. I found myself working stooped over, peering into file cabinets.

The problem suggested a system of pigeonholes, labeled with common sense names, in which one could sort transactions. This is essentially what conventional accounting accomplishes. Sorting the transaction documents themselves would eliminate the debit and credit concepts that people found so confusing. I fashioned a sort box and labeled some of the compartments with titles that matched those in conventional accounting.

The most feared part of accounting to small business people was dealing with taxes. The response was to label other compartments on the sort box with the titles found on the tax form used by most small businesses. That helped the novice see the connection between the 12th month income statement and the year-end tax return. After working the bugs out of several versions of this sort box, *No Entry Accounting*™ was ready to test in the marketplace.

Market Testing

It is the consumers in the marketplace who have the final say on whether a new product or service has sucessfully completed the design stage and is in its final form. What consumers think and feel about a product is extremely valuable information that is difficult, and therefore costly, to gather. I devised a strategy that would gather some of this valuable information without draining start-up capital. I found a few area businesses that liked the idea enough to pay for the system. In exchange for a full retail price, on-site training was included at no cost. The results of the test were rewarding, but mixed. The businesses gladly provided reference letters speaking in glowing terms as to the viability of the system. This confirmed the marketplace need for the new product.

But the market test revealed problems with product construction. The first two customers received wooden sort boxes. My supplier gave me a break on these prototypes--unit cost was just $30--but the price didn't come down with a volume order for the parts to make 20 boxes. Assembling and staining the boxes drove unit cost to $60. Some prospects seemed very interested in the system until they saw these sort boxes. They were too big, and to some prospects they were downright ugly. Some prospects would not close a sale because they had no space to store the sort box when it was not in use. Also, the name for each compartment had been placed inside the back cover. It was too hard to read. Users had to peer into each compartment to read the title. It required entirely too much effort and more lighting than was usually available.

A single market research experiment revealed problems with production cost that threatened profitability and design flaws that jeopardized usability and sale of the finished product. Without this knowledge, a clear understanding of a consumer problem and need by themselves would not be enough to ensure a business victory. Interviewing system users revealed what turned out to be final design specifications--a small, attractive cardboard box that was easy to read, use and store. Production costs were low enough to ensure profit.

Improving Marketability Through Test Marketing

With consumer need and product design understood, it was time to focus on the usability of the system. The local high school offered a ready and no-cost supply of test subjects and the opportunity to test the level of education required to learn the system. High school juniors picked up the method in just three classes. Another interesting finding was that eight of 10 students in the class had already given some thought to one day owning their own business--an insight into the future size of the market.

The next step was reaching potential customers en masse. Since all small businesses work with banks, I called upon my bank's vice president of marketing. The banker was instantly taken with the simplicity of the invention.

"I've been looking for years for a way to make teaching accounting simple," said the banker. "Our small business clients really need something like this." The banker arranged a seminar that was attended by 27 small company owners, 52 people in all.

The seminars revealed the need for a basic manual with a case study that would allow everyone in the seminar to work on the same problem together. In a single, intense day seminar attendees were now able to learn enough to implement *No Entry Accounting*™ in their own business. The bank was very excited about the good reviews they received from their customers. Perhaps this was the mechanism through which the system could be sold. But a problem developed.

The banks were responsibile for marketing the seminars and getting the small business owners to come. Some attendees were apparently coerced by bank personnel who believed them to be in need of cash management training. Bottom line: bankers prefer banking to marketing. Internal resistance to the marketing work brought an end to the seminars.

Chambers of commerce and community colleges seemed a logical alternative, but the same problem eventually surfaced. Accountants in the chambers of commerce felt threatened by the system and sabotaged repeat appearances. At community colleges, pressure grew from staff members and accounting instructors who didn't like "competing with outsiders."

Complimentary Product Development

Often, the products and services that result from market research act as stepping stones, leading to new ways to reach other markets with the existing product. Sometimes, a new product is suggested.

Over time, several hundred systems were sold and hundreds of entrepreneurs were trained. These collective experiences provided a wealth of information about the needs, wants and shortcomings of small business. Presenting numerous seminars had crystalized a series of basic business concepts. It became clear that the business war stories, the seminar lecture outline, concepts devised to present the material, and the *No Entry Accounting*™ users manual, together formed the framework for a book.

Writing about the common problems facing small businesses produced a substantial manuscript that needed a publisher. This raised a market research problem. How do you find someone who will spend tens of thousands of dollars to print and market a new book? Established publishing firms offered encouraging response to the manuscript--very clever, most interesting, just what is needed, etc.--but rejected the idea because they already had a business title in print for which they wanted no competition. This focused my search for a publisher who was new to the business and had no conflicting title. The publisher was excited by the book since the company was experiencing the very problems the book addressed. A year later, the book hit the bookstores and book clubs. The publisher had a vested interest in marketing the book, and so arranged appearances on talk shows and in newspaper articles from coast to coast.

Once the Ball is Rolling, be Ready to React

The book was read by a math professor who had loaned his son money for a restaurant venture. The professor feared that he would not get his money back and was looking for a way to help his son run a business well enough to repay the loan. The professor found the *No Entry Accounting*™ system so interesting that he called me personally to learn more. I tried hard to sell the sort box materials but to no avail. The math professor had been using computers for many years and couldn't be sold on a manual system.

What had been the basis for so many sales--the low-cost simplicity of a manual system--was now working against me. The market now demanded that the system be adapted to computer software to tap into a market of 6 million personal computer users. But while converting to the new medium of computer software offered a higher price per sale and a much better return on marketing time, it raised new questions. Who could help with software development? How much money would be required? And from where would it come?

A Gift Horse

During a seminar at a community college, I was approached by Dan, a director of information systems for a division of a Fortune 500 company. He recognized the computer potential of the No Entry system and expressed a desire to become involved with such a project. Dan agreed to work on account with payment of 50 percent of the proceeds. He would receive a premium wage to work on-site as needed and be listed in the software reference manual as Technical Designer. A year and a half later, *The Small Business Total Information System* was copyrighted. That time allowed ample testing of the system design. As with the *No Entry Accounting*™ system, development money had been obtained by selling the system in niches where finished pieces were all the buyer needed. There was a ready willingness from small business owners to accept an incomplete product in exchange for as much technical support as required.

The Company in Place

Nine years later, there are *No Entry Accounting*™ books in bookstores and libraries across the country. The No Entry manual materials have been ordered by mail and telephone from 38 states and England. Before beta testing is even complete, *The Small Business Total Information System* has been delivered in seven states. The next step was to research the marketability of the software product in computer stores and in the mail, as well as through numerous cold calls to area businesses. That research defined the next niche and the problem to be addressed.

The Next Problem

Once again it was time to define a problem and identify another consumer need:

> *The vast majority of small business computer owners loath learning from the thousands of pages of literature required to run personal computers.*

Sub Problems
1. Razor thin retail markups, rampant discounting, and inability to present a full marketing case for the product make conventional retailing an unattractive marketing outlet for a new software package.
2. The greatest demand in the marketplace is for help purchasing hardware and getting a new business system operational.

Solution
Sell *The Small Business Total Information System* only through licensed dealers who, while deriving some revenue from its sale, will primarily benefit from providing the on-site assistance required by today's small business.

Using market research techniques to define a problem, market need and product design are crucial to getting your house in order. Yet for all the effort, it is but the first step in achieving the understanding that the entrepreneur must have to survive. The next requirement is insight into the bigger picture--the economic landscape on which you will set up shop. The forces at work here are powerful enough to defeat even the most well-defined need and product. But like battling any force larger than ourselves, the key is understanding its ebb and flow and knowing when to move with it rather than foolishly standing in its path.

Barriers and Battlefields

Chapter Two

READING THE ECONOMIC LANDSCAPE

When creating a business, a basic feel for the economic climate is crucial to avoid unnecessary risks. Here's a way to get these forces on your side. The prime rate, the interest rate banks charge their best clients, is a valuable tool for the small business person. A look at the prime rate curve from 1967 to the present reveals a piece of the entrepreneurial puzzle that is nearly always overlooked. *(See Figure 1.)* Namely, how to stay afloat long enough to become successful with your business. The frequency of the peaks represents the length of time required for a good economy to slump and rebound again. Take a closer look at the periods of 1971-76, 1976-86, and 1986-91. The chance of success is enhanced by borrowing at the bottom and paying the money back before the curve turns down again.

Barriers and Battlefields

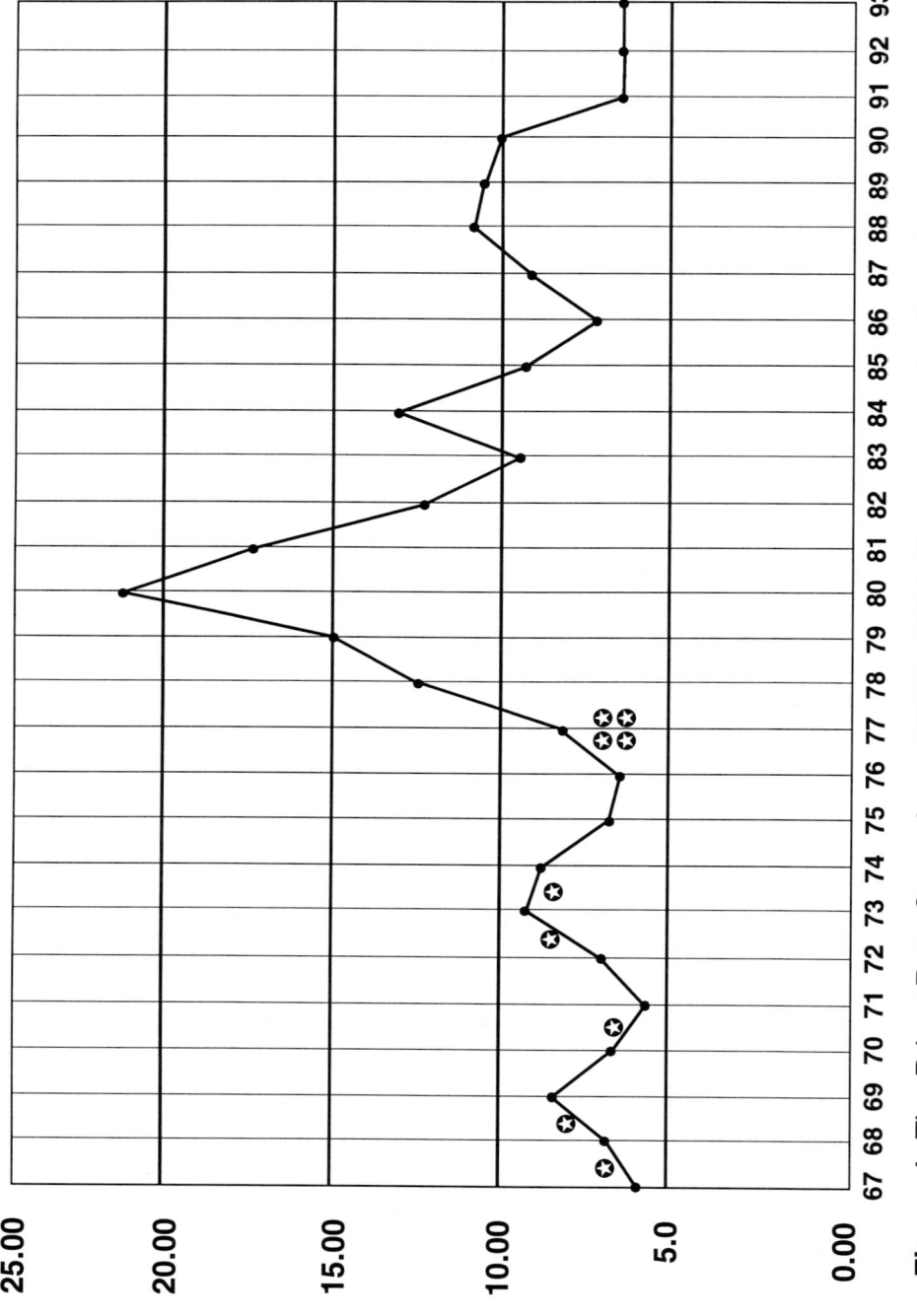

Figure 1. The Prime Rate Curve from 1967 to 1993. Every startup business is impacted by the peak-to-valley cycles. The stars indicate accounting firm startups cited on page 15.

A rising curve generally suggests an expanding economy in which demand for money is growing from a reasonable base. Consumers are spending money and new businesses are being created to meet new needs. The downward lines of the curve generally represent times when the money supply is greater than the demand, thus the lending rate declines. Overall spending is in a decline and fewer businesses are required to meet the needs of fewer spenders. Competition ensues for a dwindling market and available cash tightens.

Available collateral (property surrendered to a lender to cover an unpaid loan) is typically exhausted as business drives growth on the upside of the curve. Financing for growth and inflation on the up side of the curve is easy because assets used for collateral appreciate with a rise in prices. More collateral from the same asset is the result. On the down side of the curve, the reverse is true. The declining value of assets, plus uncertainty as to how deep a decline may go, serves to reduce the collateral value of assets.

A down side prime rate curve, then, indicates declining sales and often a lower mark-up. Lower sales indicate that less cash is available. Less cash means a loan may not get paid down. The drain on cash from interest remains constant while available cash dwindles. The net result is that high interest rate loans linger for years after a peak is reached as interest expense drains the life blood of the business--cash.

Recovery Time

The number of years in which the curve is on the down side is a measure of the time it takes consumers and businesses to pare down enough debt to once again generate surplus cash. New plans are made, new equipment is purchased, vacations are taken, etc., and so the cycle renews itself. With the addition of two factors, the value of understanding the prime rate curve becomes clear.

First, small business failure rates suggest that eight of 10 business startups fail in the first five years. Secondly, approximately 65 percent of failed businesses were profitable when they went under. Enter the entrepreneurial paradox.

Arrival Of Success, The Entrepreneurial Paradox

That statistical data uses five years as the time frame to measure new business failure is no coincidence. Whether a business will survive is determined by its condition at this five-year mark, a point we will call the "arrival of success." The arrival of success is the point at which owning a business is no longer just the purchase of a job. It is at this point when the typical business moves into the realm of becoming a profitable, taxpaying entity. It begins to contribute cash to its owner beyond what the individual could earn as someone's employee. By this time, startup costs have typically been written off and the bulk of depreciation has been taken. Family write offs such as itemized deductions and personal exemptions can no longer shelter income. Success, which carries a significant tax burden, has arrived. Yet, the cash required to pay off startup and growth-imposed debt likely is still significant.

The Triple Threat

The combination of outstanding debt (which takes cash), increased tax burden (which takes cash), and the point in time at which these converge on the prime rate curve, are the three most significant factors in determining whether a given business will survive the five-year mark. If you and your business arrive at this juncture with the curve approaching or at a peak, the cost of borrowing can be many percentage points above a safe operational level.

The most extreme example is the 1980 peak. The recession of the late Eighties and early Nineties was due in large part to the high level of debt taken on in the inflationary boom of 1977-79. Those who obtained cash near the peak borrowed at a high rate just as the business environment began to slide into a declining market. The extra burden of high interest rates, combined with declining income from a slumping marketplace, effectively prevented loans from being paid down. Businesses failed because of this extra burden, thus a significant portion of the debt was uncollectable.

Many of those who survived did so by paying only the interest on their debt. The result was that much of this debt lingered well into the Eighties. Discretionary cash and collateral were tied up with high interest rates and inflated collateral values as though locked in granite. The chart shows it took 10 years, 1976-86, for the cycle to come full circle.

The genuine profit of a typical small business is around 3 percent. (*Warning: sole proprietorship, partnership and Sub S include profit and an owner's wage together. Subtract your reasonable wage before computing profit for these entities.*) It doesn't take much to eat up 3 percent with a new loan or existing debt extended at a higher rate. Profit, your only source of cash from which loans can be paid, is quickly consumed.

Consider the math behind this concept:

3 percent profit from $100,000 in sales = $3,000

a $30,000 loan at 10 percent = $3,000
or
a $20,000 loan at 15 percent = $3,000

Unless this loan is for some item that can immediately produce additional cash profit, this new $3,000 demand upon your business will consume all of the $3,000 in free, unencumbered cash the business was generating. The owner will be funding business operations from his salary instead of cash generated by the business. Note that a loan equal to just 20 to 30 percent of annual sales is enough to turn available cash to a minus condition, leaving no cash to pay down the loan. Thus, the interest expense lingers and may consume the business if the loan is called in by the lender.

The Problem

The problem is that few small businesses are launched according to any plan, much less a blueprint that spans a single prime rate cycle. It is important not to borrow money without a plan to get you through the next peak.

The Incubator for Small Business Startups

The highest success rate is for businesses that begin at the bottom of a cycle. A case in point is an accounting franchiser which spawned 265 small accounting practices serving more than 26,000 businesses nationwide. The businesses were dependent upon a growing source of new business clients. Many of the new accounts were purchased from the sales force on finance contracts. As such, the franchiser and its small businesses were heavily dependent upon interest rates. The stars on the prime rate chart indicate the inception dates of all the accounting practices that had reached the success level of serving 200 small business clients monthly.

In the early Eighties, these businesses began to experience an extreme cash crunch. Money borrowed on the upside curve at high interest rates had to be repaid at a time when profits were down in the declining market that followed the 1980 prime rate peak. Tax was also due on profits from inflated sales dollars.

All 200 account practices had reached discretionary cash stability before the lengthy economic downturn and therefore survived. All started with interest rates on the order of 7 percent. The parent company did not. It was taken over by creditors in the mid-Eighties when it could no longer generate sufficient cash to keep its doors open. The creditors called in their loans. An excellent business idea, which had become a profitable and taxpaying small business generator, did not or could not plan it's cash use through a major peak to valley cycle. That failure was a fatal mistake.

Now is the Time

The Nineties are primed for another run of successful small business inceptions. The initial outlook is for steady, reasonable growth from what is sure to be the bottom for the foreseeable future. The preceding, long downturn has caused families and businesses to retool debt and spending to recover from the effects of years with no discretionary cash. In my opinion, the most likely scenario for the period to the year 2000 is for the prime rate curve to develop much like the decade of 1967-77. It should be a period of slow, sensible, steady growth that, like our example, should foster the equivalent of many new 200-unit accountant practices.

It is an excellent period in which to draft your action plan and get started. This is the area in the curve during which to borrow as much as you can reasonably pay off before the next peak, conservatively four years, perhaps as long as six years. The objective is not to spend lavishly, but to build a business with low operating costs that is free of debt and can generate a maximum amount of discretionary cash by the time the next peak arrives.

Your plan must include ways to considerably constrict your need for cash with the approach of a new peak. Fix used equipment instead of buying new if the payments on new might last into the next peak. Manage growth in an existing facility instead of making a long-term cash commitment to a new one. Resist hiring that extra pair of hands. You will find that the 80 percent failure rate of new businesses exists only because of ignorance. Make an effort to stay informed and do the hard things when it is necessary, even though those around you will certainly resist. You will be planning not only your business, but your way to a secure and free lifestyle.

Chapter Three

THE ALTERNATIVE TO BORROWING

Undoubtedly, the most common obstacle facing the entrepreneur is the lack of startup cash. There are strategies to overcome this problem that offer the small business person not only cash, but a litmus test of his entrepreneurship as well. A few concepts to consider:

- Develop equity to enhance borrowing power

- Begin with selected customers

- Use borrowed equipment and/or facilities

- Obtain pay-from-proceeds investors

- Psychic income

Developing Equity to Enhance Borrowing Power

The most common way to build equity is purchasing a home. The difference between market value of the home and the mortgage due is the collateral value. Collateral is converted to cash by borrowing against this equity. Lenders look favorably upon residence collateral. An entrepreneur's willingness to collateralize his home on a business venture speaks well of his confidence in being able to repay the loan. The value of this type of collateral is most likely to remain stable or increase, which makes it sought after tender for longer-term financing.

There are many ways to develop collateral that do not require owning a home. Joe, for example, has a knack for tinkering with things. As he drives home from work on garbage collection day, he often sees discarded appliances waiting to be hauled to the dump. One day a lawnmower that looked to be in reasonable shape caught his eye, so he stopped to pick it up. Upon closer examination he discovered that it could easily be repaired. A couple hours of labor and chasing for parts would yield a good lawnmower that could sell for perhaps $150. Joe purchased the parts for only $20. He managed to increase his equity by $130 simply by repairing a discarded mower. Even if the total time spent on the piece was three hours, he increased his equity by $50 dollars an hour. Best of all, by selling the mower he converted this new equity directly to cash.

A week later, Joe saw a washing machine and, later, a dryer. He hauled both pieces home and used a portion of his lawnmower cash to buy the parts to repair and repaint the units. It took only a weekend to sell, deliver and install the matching set for $400. Over time, Joe was able in his free time to fund the development of what eventually grew to become an appliance service and resale business.

Moving Up

Let's apply Joe's technique on a larger scale. Tom was competing for an available trucking contract with a local quarry. However, off loading pallets of stone required a boom truck. A new boom truck would cost more than $80,000, far more than Tom could afford. His only collateral was the used dump truck he owned. It was valued at $3,500, but would also be required to service the contract.

Tom shopped unsuccessfully for a used boom truck. But he did find a used boom that could be mounted on a truck. More shopping turned up an old truck that could be modified to permit installation of the used boom. Tom then found a used truck center that would refurbish the truck and assemble the parts. Assembled and refurbished, the boom truck would have a market value of at least $12,000. Yet the separate parts and assembly would cost only $6,500.

The enhanced value of the refurbished truck was $5,500. ($12,000 market value less $6,500 assembly cost.) With the $3,500 collateral in his dump truck, Tom had $9,500 in collateral to finance a $6,500 loan with which to pay for the boom truck.

At the bank, Tom found that his 146 percent collateral on used equipment was only marginally acceptable. He could be assured of a loan only if his application included a multi-year contract with the quarry. Tom negotiated a five-year, exclusive contract that more than covered repayment of the loan. Over the years that followed, the low overhead afforded by used equipment, and the revenue assured by the exclusive multi-year contract, created a major small business success story.

Begin with Selected Customers

Customers can be a form of collateral. As the customer base grows, it can be used to lower startup costs. Sue the hairstylist wanted to open a salon, but had no cash to buy equipment. It occurred to her that many people might prefer having their hair styled in their homes, especially older people for whom travel is difficult. By word of mouth, she let it be known that for competitive prices she would make house calls. By working in the customer's home, she was able to earn a competitive fee without overhead. Of course, there was the inconvenience of not having professional sinks and dryers, but the customers obviously valued the convenience more and did not mind. There was the cost and time of travel, but careful planning could allow for those factors. For example, Sue landed a regularly scheduled visit to a retirement center, where she could serve several clients in a single trip.

Gradually, Sue accumulated enough cash to convert part of her home into a salon. She could now add to her clientele those customers who prefer the social ambiance of going out to get their hair done. In a few years, Sue acquired enough clients to move the business from the house to a commercial salon. The equipment and fixtures she had accumulated served to decrease her start-up cash needs. Sue was able to convert her satisfied customer base into full-time entrepreneurship with only a small amount of additional cash. She didn't even need a loan.

Borrowed Equipment and Facilities

Even a small client base, when teamed with borrowed equipment and facilities, can generate the cash needed to create self employment. Jane was a great cook, and over the years developed a collection of wonderful recipes. Friends regularly urged her to write a book of her recipes and the special cooking techniques she had developed. Jane had the necessary writing skills, but not the cash to purchase a computer and word processing software. She knew that without the system, a book project was not practical.

During a visit to the public library, she noticed several computer systems available free to library district residents. Coincidentally, her friend Martha had mentioned that she needed some writing done, but didn't have the skills and would have to hire out the work.

The free use of a computer system and a writing job at hand clicked in Jane's mind. She could charge a very reasonable price for the job and use the library system to perform the work. The deal fell together. Jane was able to begin earning money toward her own computer and Martha got a bargain on her word processing needs. In only a few months, Jane was able to land enough word processing work to buy her own entry-level system. From there, she became self-employed by using her computer system to write and market her recipe book.

Paying from the Proceeds

Another cashless way to start a business is paying for overhead from the proceeds of a job. Mark wanted to start an auto repair shop but had no garage and only a few of the required tools. A friend owned a garage with some of the basic tools, such as a commercial jack, a power outlet for a welder, etc. Mark proposed a unique rent arrangement.

The rent was based upon a percentage of the gross from each repair job. In this way, Mark needed cash for rent only if he had income. By taking only those jobs for which he had the necessary tools, he kept his cash needs to a minimum. By buying additional tools cheaply at garage sales and auctions, he created the same effect as having enough cash to buy new, higher-priced tools. Gradually, he collected many of the expensive, seldom-used tools that permitted him to take on larger, more profitable jobs.

Mark built his client base and collection of tools to the point at which he could offer his friend a fixed monthly rent. Together, Mark and his friend negotiated a rent/option-to-buy agreement that resulted in the profitable sale of an otherwise unused garage and the development of a successful auto repair business.

Psychic Income

My own experience with this type of cashless financing came while developing my *Small Business Information System,* the computer version of *No Entry Accounting*™. I had considerable experience designing computer systems, but didn't feel confident writing my own program code. Because of the success of my first book, *The Small Business Survival Guide*, and sales of the *No Entry Accounting*™ system, I was able to attract the attention of a highly-skilled programmer whose regular job left him available to work on evenings and weekends. To get him involved, I offered a higher-than-average hourly rate in exchange for him accepting payment only from proceeds of future sales. If the product sells, he will be in a position to earn 30 percent more than the salary at his regular job.

More than the potential earnings, it was psychic income that probably contributed most to his coming on board. Psychic income is the pleasure one feels by being involved in an exciting, challenging, or especially worthwhile project. It can also come from the hope of substantial gain if things work out to their fullest potential. This project provided examples of both types. First, there was the hope of being on the ground floor of what might become a highly-successful small business software package. Second, was the possibility of national recognition in his profession by having his name included in the reference manual as providing technical support. In this case, psychic income may well have been worth more than the 130 percent salary gain. Whatever the outcome, he will have gained broad ranging experience in systems development to list on his resume and contribute to his future income.

The process of funding small business development serves a broader purpose than generating cash. It is a litmus test of an individual's ability and desire to do what is necessary to make a small business succeed. The greater one's flexibility, creativity and personal initiative in handling cash problems, the greater the chance of success.

PART TWO

THE INFORMATION BARRIER

Chapter Four

DECIDING WHEN TO COMPUTERIZE

The typical small business decision to computerize is seldom based on cold, hard business logic. Too often, a system is purchased before the tasks to be performed are determined. Or the entrepreneur attaches to computers an almost magical power to make everything they touch faster and more efficient.

The result is computers lying around, some components in their original packaging material, with others unpacked but stored unceremoniously in a dark, unused, back corner of the building. These business owners bought a computer before they identified their real needs, and before they researched whether a computer could, in fact, solve their company's particular problems. Even if the computer is a regularly used tool for the business, the entrepreneur may have fallen victim to the marketing and sales promotion traps laid by manufacturers and purchased more system than was needed to serve the company. That overspent cash will never be recovered in a used equipment market driven ever downward by falling prices for new gear.

The key to successfully adding a computer to a new business is identifying a threshold system--just enough hardware and software to perform a clearly defined set of tasks at the lowest cost possible. Before we turn our attention to the glossary of computer terms that will identify such a system, let's look at other issues with which the entrepreneur must first grapple.

System Installations

We need to put into perspective the scope of the task involved. Most everyone has experienced purchasing some simple device such as a barbecue grill, a bicycle or a swing set. The instructions to get the things assembled usually fit on an 11-by-17 sheet of paper folded into four standard pages. Then there is the parts list, the warranty, and sometimes a simple manual on safe operation. I personally have purchased all three items and must confess that it took me half a day to assemble a working swing set one bright Saturday. My background at the time included mechanical drawing, years working with schematic drawings and blueprints, and considerable experience with tools.

The Big, Small Machine

Compared to the most complicated swing set, even a small computer system is a big machine. Consider the technological advances that have made this big machine available to every small business owner. Just 23 years ago I was selling "entry level" computer systems for $80,000. Today, I write on a computer system that two years ago cost $2,000. The $80,000 system provided 16,000 characters of core memory for high-speed processing of program instructions, could store 2.3 million characters of data and printed at the speed of 87 lines--about 2.5 pages--per minute. My personal computer offers four million characters of high-speed memory, can store 40 million characters of data (which can be doubled with a single piece of inexpensive software) and prints four pages per minute. The $80,000 system filled a small room that required climate control and anti-static carpeting. My system sits on a desktop. More often than not, I use a laptop unit that fits in a briefcase. The old unit required a highly-trained sales force, supported by a highly-trained field engineering force, both of which were supported by a highly-trained software support team. The new unit comes with none of that.

But, when we look at what the new computer systems *do* require, we begin to understand the giant leap the entrepreneur must make to move into computerization. Unlike the swing set with its four pages of instruction and a parts list of a few nuts and bolts, this computer system requires more than **3,000** pages of technical support literature.

Like the frazzled parent wrestling with the swing set, many venture into the world of computers with but a basic set of skills such as reading ability, limited experience with simple tools, and maybe some very limited exposure to the logic behind these complex machines.

The Paper Chase

Let's begin with the hardware--the things we can touch, such as the monitor, keyboard, diskettes and processor. My modest system comes with a 1.2-inch thick stack of technical information on the use of the various components. It describes how to hook the system together, turn it on, and use its esoteric features. It even tells me how to diagnose problems when it needs a field engineer. I use inches to describe the quantity of printed material because the page numbering starts over with each new chapter. This keeps you from finding out how many pages you must read to finish the book. In a conventionally numbered book, 1.2 inches would be anywhere from 500 to 700 pages depending upon paper thickness.

Each package of software comes with such documentation. Many systems include DOS, a program that controls the operation of the hardware and permits the operator to communicate with the machine--approximately 700 pages. Also commonplace is Windows, a program that permits DOS to communicate through visual images, more like people do--another 800 pages. Since I am not that great of a computer programmer, I have installed Excel. This spreadsheet program lets even inexperienced people perform basic programming functions without knowing much about actual programming. It comes with three manuals--640, 353, and 535 pages. Writing requires me to have sophisticated word processing software. The operations manuals include four 100-page booklets and a manual of 849 pages. Adding insult to injury are 500-page books such as "Windows for Dummies" and "Excel for Dummies" that allow consumers to use the programs more effectively. And that's not the end of it. Making a new computer system dovetail with your plan for operating a business adds a whole new layer of complexity. Let's consider a case history.

Dreams vs. Practical Reality

One day I visited a small, family-owned and operated manufacturer. Business was good and the family members wanted to install a computer system. Each individual was wildly enthusiastic and full of ideas for the system.

"I should be able to get a report on my orders that ties into these various jobs we are doing," said one son.

"I want to be able to bring up a list that shows me how much we charge for these various operations," said another.

"Mom wants to do the payroll, billing and write the accounts payable checks."

"Can we do these little brochures?"

"We would like to cut our accounting bill by preparing financial statements in house."

In a matter of minutes, their collective requests required all the manuals mentioned above plus perhaps another 1,000 pages in technical support literature for the specific applications they wanted to use. And then mom said, "Will you come in and show us how to turn it on and all that stuff?" And the sons said, "And we need to learn how to type." No problem! Just throw in another 70 or 80 pages for a basic typing tutorial. But that assumes you already know how to use the computer, learn well from reading and have a couple of months free to learn all this.

On the opposite end of the spectrum from those who want to instantly computerize every business operation are those who ignore their information needs for too long. Frequently, I encounter small business owners who have avoided computerization for so long that they have reached the point at which they feel they must start out with a huge, complex system--multiple input stations connected by data communications linkups. They must begin with fully-integrated systems that connect every conceivable use of the system from day one. Some of the businesses are 24-hour operations. No one seems to have time to learn how to use the system because there is always more important work at hand. This approach is absolutely wrong! Don't wait until a booming business forces computerization upon you. The risks are simply too great. Begin with a simple, comprehensive system that can be supported by a few reference manuals. The transition to grander computerization is easier if you begin with a system that will let you pull the plug and restart if you make a big mistake.

Fiscally Expedient Compromise

The cost of computer hardware and all these various software components is already fiscally expedient. After all, if a $300 program is designed to do in minutes what it took Ben Franklin a month to do with his printing press, that is a good rate of return. But fiscal expedience is often lost when it is time to actually use a system which is comprised of so many complicated pieces. I have seen thousands of small businesses with computer gear left to gather dust in the back room, some of the equipment still in the original box. The problem is always the same. They couldn't get the darn thing running sufficiently that the time spent at the machine could generate any productive business gain. What good is spending $2,000 to do in minutes what took Ben Franklin a month if you can't actually do it? The $2,000 expenditure is just so much more "potential"--like many other things small business owners purchase and never use effectively.

Start Small, But Comprehensive

As you move toward computerization--and surely you must, regardless of the complexity--choose the computer setup from which you will gain the most at the outset. To my mind, the small business person gains the most from preparation of his own financial statements, particularly, how to prepare an income statement. As I detailed in my first book, *"The Small Business Survival Guide,"* the purpose is to improve one's ability to proficiently manage cash. Buying a computer can provide the initial gain. Many small businesses pay $100 or $200 a month for accounting services. The entire computer package described above can be leased for less than $100 per month. Preparing financial statements in house makes buying a computer expedient if you do nothing more than reduce your accounting bill by $100 per month. However, if your business is still very small in terms of transaction volume, and accounting is still an in-house task of an hour or two a month, the purchase of a computer system to manage cash may not be fiscally expedient.

Most computer applications do not have such clear cut gains. Computerized inventory, for example, usually mandates procedures which are not part of existing manual systems. The cost of work required at the outset to fill voids in the manual system cannot be recouped with immediate gains. These gains must come from better buying decisions in the future, better job estimating and perhaps more efficient flow of labor and materials. Each of these benefits requires a short-term investment in the form of cash paid to employees who are training on the system instead of generating revenue, as well as your extra labor and learning time. My own experience shows that the sum of these additional expenses quickly exceeds the cost of purchasing computer hardware, but is seldom accounted for at the outset. Yet another computer dilemma is how to quickly cut through as much of the mountain of reference material as is necessary to finally use the computer to get the job done.

On-Site Training

Here is the tough bullet to bite. Most businesses large and small cannot bring themselves to take their computer purchase to the logical conclusion. The end goal is to get the system fully operational in the minimum amount of time. The objective must be to recover ALL the expenses involved in computerizing. Know this: The "high" one experiences after buying his first computer, with all it's magical bells and whistles, vanishes in the instant one realizes the mountain of work and knowledge required to make it all work. This realization is what sends so many small business systems to the back corner of a dark closet.

To prevent this failure, the entrepreneur purchasing a computer system must be willing to budget an amount double the cost of hardware for training. This strategy has two distinct advantages. It ensures the full and rapid deployment of the entire system. And it provides protection against the temptation to buy into exotic computer features that you don't know for certain you will ever use. The spending limit imposed by budgeting for training will tend to curtail impulsive spending on hardware and software. By bringing in an outside trainer knowledgeable on the software you have purchased, you essentially purchase a guide through thousands of pages you need not read to get your system fully operational. The end savings can be dramatic and may prevent you losing your business to the process of computerizing.

Don't skimp on the number of people trained to run the system. It is a false sense of security that comes from thinking that only you or a single employee need be trained. The process of putting so much knowledge in the hands of so few people is contrary to the logic of successful business operations. Responsibility, authority, and the performance of unique and valuable tasks need to be dispersed across the small business environment. Most of us start out as the chief cook and bottle washer out of necessity. We must do it all because there is no one else. But the sooner our fledgling enterprises have the opportunity to disperse portions of the entrepreneurial load, the sooner our business can become truly successful. A quickly-installed, fully-operational computer system can be a valuable link in the chain of events leading to entrepreneurial success.

Chapter Five

THE THRESHOLD BUSINESS COMPUTER SYSTEM

With pre-purchase issues addressed, we can identify a small business threshold system. It includes application software, system software, computer hardware, training, and the specific needs of the small business. The threshold system will meet all the needs of the vast majority of small businesses. It is readily identifiable and affordable for most everyone who is genuinely in business. The key concepts:

- The automatic transmission
- The need for speed
- Accomplishing the required speed
- Mass storage memory, the hard drive
- Avoiding the boat anchor

Barriers and Battlefields

The Automatic Transmission

Just as the manual transmission is favored only by automotive purists and collectors, so it is with the computer's operating system. Only purists and hobbyists should spend their time with the old manual method of learning computer languages and memorizing commands that must be typed in each time they are to be executed. The only logical choice for the small business person is a computer with an "automatic transmission"--System 7.5 on the Macintosh and Windows on IBM compatibles. These "automatic" operating systems (the language understood by the program brain of the computer) far exceed the capabilities of the manual operating systems of old. This is especially true in the area of making the computer accessible for the average person with no formal computer education. The gains made in the transition from manual to automatic transmission are even more dramatic in computers than autos.

In both instances, the automatic transmission is considerably more complicated to design and maintain. But as with the automobile, the driver need not be concerned with that. Just as with autos, the performance of a computer with an automatic operating system is less efficient than its manual counterpart. But recent trends are offsetting this. The price of computer hardware has fallen rapidly, while the speed of operation has improved dramatically. This combination has allowed computer manufacturers to effectively mask the increased complexity and inefficiency of the automatic, and still decrease the price. The result is computer technology available to the small business owner that is so accessible it can rightfully be called "user friendly." The new technology represents a quantum cut in learning time and required ability for the computer user.

The Need for Speed

The need for computing speed arises from the various layers of hidden steps that make up a single command to perform a given task. Say, for example, you have an invoice on the screen of your computer. When you enter a part number, you want the computer to display a description of the product on your screen.

The process begins when your application program recognizes that you have finished entering the part number through the keyboard. The program begins processing the data. The application program passes the data to a programming tool such as a spreadsheet like Excel. The spreadsheet performs its function and passes the data to the system software.

System software is the program brain of the computer and it varies by vendor. Again, Macintosh calls its software System 7. IBM-compatible PCs use two pieces. The manual transmission is DOS. The automatic transmission add-on is called Windows. System software prepares data for entry into the hardwired components of the computer. The part number is located in processor memory or on a disk drive. The process is then reversed, resulting in a part description being displayed on the screen.

Each component in the chain of events works most effectively in its own language. It is as if the application software speaks English, the programming tool uses French, the system software is in German, and the machine components have a language all their own. As the request for part number information passes through the various layers, each component requires time to translate instructions and perform them.

The operating system, for example, needs time to interpret the French message sent to it by the programming tool, perform its portion of the task, and finally translate its work into the language of the machine components.

While this concept is easily grasped, it is a time-consuming, bit-by-bit process. Each letter you type on the keyboard, for example, requires eight bits to describe. Each number requires four bits. Just as the revolutions of the hands of a clock perform the function of keeping time, the revolutions, or cycles, of a computer processor perform computer logistics. Even when a computer processor is humming along at 10 million such cycles per second, some functions appear to bring the system to a halt.

Difficulty in Achieving Real Gain

Our search for a part description encounters other limitations which hinder the rapid processing of data. The disk drive on which the part number is stored, for example, is capable of operating speeds measured in thousandths of a second rather than the millionths of a second the processor can achieve. Millions of electronic processor cycles are wasted as the disk chugs along in its mechanical search for the part number. Millions more cycles are required to pass through the various interpretive layers of software. The result is an operator sitting idly by, waiting for the appropriate part description to appear on screen. Depending on the computer system, it could take 30 minutes to prepare an invoice that would require only 10 minutes on the typewriter, or perhaps only two minutes written by hand on a preprinted form.

Barriers and Battlefields

Reaching the Required Speed

Random Access Memory, or RAM, is high-speed processing memory. The information in it exists as long as the computer is running. Accidentally turn off power to the machine and the data in RAM will be lost. Think of RAM like the countertop of a workbench. The computer uses it as a place to set down the tools it has pulled out of the toolbox to do a job. While a tool may not be in use at the moment, it will be needed shortly to finish the task.

All the interpretive layers in a software application are the tools that, together, perform a function. Applications programs and all the interpretive layers of software can now be executed in this high-speed memory. If there is sufficient RAM to store an entire program and all the interpretive layers at one time, the program will run at maximum efficiency.

If the total memory required for programs is larger than the available RAM--which is nearly always the case--the operating system software breaks the programs into pieces that fit into available RAM. Processor cycles are wasted as the computer accesses the slow mechanical memory to swap in and out of RAM the necessary pieces of each program. Using our tool analogy, time is wasted as the computer goes back and forth exchanging tools between the toolbox and the countertop.

To place a complete small business information system into RAM could require 2 Megabytes (M). Where one byte equals one letter, a megabyte is 1 million letters. DOS and Windows may take 10M or more. Tools like Excel can take another 10M. That's 22M of RAM at a time when systems typically come with two to four megabytes of RAM. Advances in computer manufacture have dramatically cut the cost of installing additional memory, but 22M of RAM is still a lot from a price perspective. Therefore, we need to accomplish a gain in speed by more economical means.

Processor Clock Speed

One method computer manufacturers use to more efficiently run large programs in limited RAM space is to increase the speed of the processor clock. Clock speeds range from 8 million cycles per second (a rest mode for a notebook computer) to 60 million cycles per second for the widely-available 486 processor. Clock speed makes a tremendous difference in the ability to effectively operate large programs. Keep in mind, however, that gains are wasted if system peripherals, such as the disk drive or printer, cannot respond to the increased speed.

Data Handled in a Single Clock Cycle

Still another method for souping up a system is increasing the amount of data a processor can handle on a single clock cycle. Most of the current processors handle 16 bits--roughly two letters--at a time. More powerful processors handle 32 bits, or four letters, at a time. This method also makes a tremendous difference in the ability to handle large programs effectively. For example, a 386/40 processor (a model 386 with a 40 million cycles per second clock) can outrun a newer, low-end 486 processor. That's because the 386 processes 32 bits per cycle while the basic 486 processes only 16 bits per cycle.

The Need for Mass Storage

Software programs must be stored inside the computer on the hard disk. The documents we create can be stored there too, or on diskettes. Sophisticated programs can require large chunks of mass storage space. Word processing programs commonly range from 8 to 15 megabytes. A good spreadsheet program may require 10M and more. The computer's operating system itself can take between 8 and 50 megabytes. For a typical small business, these requirements and necessary application software can be stored in a 40 megabyte hard drive. (Graphics programs eat lots of memory, and will push hard drive minimum requirements well beyond the 40M entry level system.) Should your hard drive fill quickly, have no fear. Widely available are software packages, such as Stacker, that double the storage space of the hard drive.

The Threshold System

When we translate all this into a computer configuration, buying a computer for the small business is easy. A 386/20 processor with 4 megabytes of RAM and a 40 megabyte hard drive is all 95 percent of small businesses will ever need. This is sufficient to effectively handle currently available programs such as Excel, a word processor or a basic desktop publisher, and business applications. The hardware for such a system, including a letter quality printer, is under $1,200. A sophisticated word processor, a spreadsheet such as Excel, and a good set of applications programs can add another $800 to $1,000. Hardware prices are falling and will do so with each new generation of products. Computer Assisted Design users, high-end desktop publishers and users with color graphic needs, may want to begin with 8M of RAM, a 200 megabyte hard drive and a model 486 processor.

The Boat Anchor

There is no sorrier sight in business than a computer abandoned in a dark corner of a back room. Remember: the specifications of the computer aren't as important as purchasing a threshold system. How much a system can do in theory isn't as important as what you quickly can learn to make it do for your business. Don't buy low-priced computer hardware in the mistaken belief that you have computerized your company. Hardware--without usable software and the training it takes to make it run--is nothing more than an expensive boat anchor.

Chapter Six

THE PRINTER

Of all the peripherals one may purchase with a computer, the printer is most apt to limit the ways in which the computer is used.

While processor speed is measured in millionths of a second and disk drives in thousandths of a second, printers operate in pages per minute. A typical printer will do well to operate at four pages per minute in its production, or low-quality, mode. The better the quality and the greater the image detail, the slower a printer will operate. This is not particularly fast, especially when other factors are taken into account.

The limitations stem from several different aspects of computer use. Some key considerations when selecting a printer:

1. Your Requirements
2. Site logistics
3. Printing and forms handling
4. The impact of software and other needs

Study Your Requirements

The entrepreneur needs to look closely at his company's requirements. A case in point is writing checks.

The typical, full-time small business writes 45 checks per month. Some of these may be payroll checks. Checks may be written each day. Payroll may be limited to several checks biweekly. A portion may be written off site. The result is that there is seldom a period in which 10 or 20 checks can be written in a single pass. The lower the number in a single pass, the less beneficial the printer becomes.

Therefore, software requiring that checks be written on the computer system may waste time rather than save it. While printing may be fast, preparing the system to print may take longer than writing a check by hand. The additional expense of producing custom-printed computerized checks could also contribute to the decision to keep checks off the system.

Site Logistics

A very basic consideration in using a printer is often overlooked. That is, where will it be used? I have seen printers jammed into a crowded bottom shelf with no access to the rear of the unit. Many printers load forms from the rear, which creates a logistical hassle in this case.

Moving the printer each time the forms are changed can easily add more time to the printing operation than doing some jobs by hand. Just maneuvering a heavy box of continuous form paper into place behind a desk can be a big job. Then, feeding the paper through a hole in the desk so that it flows freely and is aligned in the printer can get tricky. Paper that does not feed easily into the rear of the printer can hang up and tear in the middle of a job. Supplies are lost, jobs must be repeated and time is wasted.

Generally, tasks that required less than 10 minutes and/or a limited number of documents may well be better performed off the computer system.

Print Registration And Form Handling

It usually takes considerable practice, even with easy access to the rear of the printer, to line up the print positions from the program with those on the actual forms. Many forms can be wasted with test runs to get the print stock to register properly. After several forms print, the name or amount may be well out of its print position, requiring the job to be reprinted.

Each time a new form is required, the user must pay the price of removing stock already in the printer, realigning, and test printing the new stock to be certain elements are aligned. Considering the range of forms that a business may use--invoices, accounts payable checks, payroll checks, accounts receivable statements, plain paper reports, gummed labels, envelopes, and perhaps letterhead stationery--the most computer work for the small business could well be getting forms in and out of the printer.

Software Requirements

Much of the problem can be eliminated by using software designed for small business. If your application program generates it's own forms, the need to frequently change paper diminishes. Invoices, accounts receivable statements, reports and perhaps letterhead stationery can be printed on plain paper.

Even envelopes can be eliminated if your software and printer can handle gummed address labels. Occasionally, a complete set can be printed or just a batch of those most frequently used. As envelopes are required, simply remove a preprinted gummed label from the sheet and paste it on an envelope. A dozen envelopes can be prepared this way in the time it takes to turn on the computer and bring up a software program with envelope addressing.

Only checks would require a change of forms. If a program is written properly, you can use the same check for both payroll and accounts payable. This eliminates an additional change.

Payroll and accounts payable checks may not be written at the same time. Accounts payable checks may be required at any time of day, for C.O.D. deliveries perhaps. Some checks may be removed from the checkbook and completed in a store or on a job site. The need for such checks can reduce or eliminate the practicality of writing accounts payable checks on the computer.

Types of Printers and Paper

Printers come in two basic types, impact and jet. Impact printers physically strike the paper to transfer each character to the paper through a ribbon cartridge. Ink, bubble, and laser jet printers work much like copiers, electrostatically fusing toner powder to the paper.

Selecting the printer type right for you could be as simple as determining the type of document you will most often need. A four part invoice, for example, can be printed in a single pass with an impact printer. Carbon or carbonless transfer paper records the printed matter on copies two three and four.

With the ink, bubble, and laser jet printers, only a single copy can be made in one pass of the document. The same invoice would require four passes by the printer since there is no penetration of multiple layers. If time does not permit four passes in your business, an impact printer may be the solution. Either way, both types can be had for around $650.

Print Quality

Each user must determine the level of print quality needed for the documents generated in his particular business. The lowest readability comes from impact printers with a small number of pins in the impact head. A nine-pin printer offers poor quality, especially on larger characters where outside curves show jagged edges. A 24-pin printer provides typewriter quality on standard type and only adequate quality for most applications with larger letters and graphics.

The jet type printers provide the best image quality, particularly on larger letters used in form headings or in graphics. Jet printers can print smooth outside curves while the impact printers, even good ones, leave noticeable corners. The inexpensive ink jet is capable of generating letter-quality copy. If your business demands camera-ready copy, you may be stuck with the higher cost and slower output of a laser jet printer.

For most small business print jobs, the quality of print is acceptable with the 24-pin printers. Many start at $200. Jet printers start at $400. The laser jets with color capability start at $750.

Printer Size

Manufacturers recently have made strides in producing portable jet printers. Some weigh only two pounds. Both the printer and a notebook computer can be carried in a briefcase. This configuration allows the user to take the entire system to the job site or on a trip. The print speed of two or three pages per minute may be all that is required for demonstrations or presentations. Back at the office, such a printer speed may be sufficient to handle accounting tasks on time. For many small businesses, the portability of such a configuration could be very valuable. Don't let the printer you purchase hamstring your system. It's an expensive part of productivity which cannot be overlooked.

PART THREE

THE BATTLE TO MANAGE RESOURCES

Chapter Seven

MONEY MANAGEMENT

Money is the lifeblood of every business. More than just the measurement of its success, the amount of cash available to a company determines how it will operate and what it can bring to the marketplace. Philosophies of how to spend entrepreneurial money are many, covering a spectrum that ranges from squandering on one extreme to hoarding on the other. Generally, very few entrepreneurs spend money wisely. Let's explore the logic behind different styles of spending money with an analogy.

Suppose you must cross a desert on foot for the first time. Obviously, water is your most precious commodity. You know from earlier travelers that one gallon of water is the bare minimum needed to complete the journey. But that gallon will satisfy only your drinking needs. It is not enough for bathing, washing dishes, or supporting any beasts you might ride or bring along. The journey is long enough to make the weight of your possessions an important factor. Carrying extra provisions will help make the journey more bearable, but their weight and the energy required to carry them increase the amount of water required. Therefore, provisions must be kept to a minimum.

Once under way, how will you know how to pace your water consumption? Will you needlessly sacrifice in the beginning only to near the end of the trip with much more water than you need, but weak from dehydration? Will you drink too quickly at first and run out before you reach the other side? What if you encounter a fellow traveler willing to trade a tasty meal and an umbrella for some of your water? What if the traveler has miscalculated his own needs and will not reach the other side if you do not share your water? What if he is so desperate he steals your water?

The questions don't stop until the journey is completed and what was once only a cursory knowledge of the trip becomes the full understanding that comes from experience. So it is with money management.

No new entrepreneur comes equipped with the experience that leads to a genuine understanding of the task at hand. We gather that from others and through study and observation. But as we will soon learn, observations, particularly those we never realize we are making, can give us a distorted view of how money should be used. So how can we avoid the types of mistakes that will prevent us from completing the journey?

The Vantage Point

Put yourself in a vantage point from which you can safely observe the traveler for his entire journey. How much water does he have? Does he have a map? Are there guideposts by which he can measure his progress and consumption of his precious water? Has he allowed for the unexpected? What compromises do you see him make as he meets a fellow traveler in the middle of the desert? Does he stay on course when confronted with choices, or does he lose sight of his goal?

Comparing the desert crossing to money management begins with the entrepreneur's knowledge of how much money he has before beginning the entrepreneurial journey. He must know how much he can raise as well as how much he has in hand. How might he be able to generate more money if a special need arises. Does he have a business plan which focuses upon the use of money? Can he monitor his use of money against the objectives of the plan? The more detailed one's money plan, the more valuable it becomes as time progresses.

The Scarcest Resource

The primary problem with money management is that it typically does not focus on money. Like water on the desert journey, money must be managed as the scarcest resource. Judy had a burning desire to own a fashion accessories shop of her own. From day one she was bombarded with choices to buy one product over another and accept this discount schedule over that one. She shopped feverishly for the best price, thinking it would keep costs to a minimum. The best price, however, was always associated with some marketing gimmick designed to generate a bigger sale for the supplier. Judy bought in large quantities to receive substantial discounts. She was elated with the money she thought she was saving.

The problem with her money management style surfaced when Judy took her first inventory. Item after item remained in it's original shipping package. A few of each item was on display, but the sale of many of these items lagged well behind what Judy had expected. Other items had sold out and needed to be reordered. But since Judy was still a new business with no payment record, her suppliers wanted cash. To reorder, she would have to come up with money she didn't have. Judy's problem was not that she didn't have enough startup money. Rather, she had tied up too much capital with her strategy of buying in quantity to get the lowest unit price. Her money was invested in slow-moving items and merchandise that didn't move at all.

The temptation to buy items on sale must be tempered by your overall plan for handling money. Buying a truckload of merchandise at a 70 percent discount is fine if it doesn't tie up your money for so long that you go out of business waiting to sell the truckload of goods. A better strategy is buying small quantities at market price and testing consumer demand. With the knowledge of what sells and what doesn't, Judy would have had the money to stock up on the movers and limited her losses on the items that were still in boxes. The key is managing money as a scarce resource rather than managing the cost of individual purchases.

The Basic Negative Impulse

After years working for a big company as a computer programmer, Tony needed a change. When an opportunity appeared to become self-employed, Tony took the plunge and started a business processing medical claims for area health clinics. Tony needed to buy his own computer system to do the job, but he had $5,000 in savings. Tony was quite familiar with computers and knew about all the latest bells and whistles and the ever-greater features that manufacturers promised were just around the corner.

Tony went computer shopping and quickly became obsessed with the possibility that upcoming products would make his purchase obsolete. As a result, Tony bought a large system capable of supporting a host of options already available as well as some that had not yet hit the market.

The purchase required all of Tony's original $5,000 and he was required to finance another $800. He felt he would quickly recover this additional money once he began processing claims. As is always the case, acquiring clients and getting a new system online required more time than Tony anticipated. Then, a more ominous problem cropped up. Tony had purchased his system for its expandability. Now that he had begun significant processing, he discovered that the hangup was not some new gadget or encroaching technical obsolescence. Tony needed a faster printer. Unfortunately, he had tapped out his original loan, so he did not have the money with which he could purchase a new printer capable of the print speed and quality he now required. He was stuck in an operation only marginally able to produce income.

Once again, bad money management had put the fate of a business up for grabs. Spending decisions were based upon bells and whistles rather than focusing upon management of a scarce resource.

Had Tony purchased a threshold system and kept some cash in hand, he could quickly have upgraded his system and even paid cash. There would have been no monthly payments on the financed portion of an overpowered system or money squandered on bells and whistles that did nothing to generate revenue. Hedging against technological obsolescence bought him nothing either, since a basic system with a faster printer would have kept him in business for the foreseeable future. Granted, he would still be out the money spent for the first printer, but it got him started and there would have been sufficient money to upgrade once he knew exactly what his new business required. His total outlay would have been less and there would have been no lingering debt.

Getting to the Other Side

The ability to see cash as the scarcest resource is crucial to successful money management. The willingness to conserve cash up front for later eventualities is a major element of successful money management. You cannot permit the impulse to save on individual items, without looking at the whole picture, to become the basis for decision-making. Do not permit compulsive and/or impulsive spending choices (newness, bells and whistles, fear of technical obsolescence, etc.) to be the basis for your spending decisions. Finally, make a plan and stick to it so that a passing traveler in the desert doesn't cause you to lose sight of the importance of your scarce resource.

Remember the gallon of water. Using it too fast doesn't work. Using it too slowly may not work. Letting outside influences guide you doesn't work. Keep focused on managing your scarcest resource as the means for getting to the other side.

Chapter Eight

ACCOUNTING

Accounting has long been considered the guiding, universal principle for entrepreneurs. The ugly paradox, however, is that conventional accounting statements are a major contributor to small business failure. Here's why:

- Sometimes, the entrepreneur spends money and it doesn't count.
- Sometimes, money that hasn't been received must count.
- The tax collector always wins.
- Conventional accounting statements cover up all of the above.

Some Expenditures Do Not Count

Not being able to record cash spent on the business is a problem, the essence of which lies in the different way transactions are indicated in *Cash Accounting* versus *Accrual Accounting*. In cash accounting, a transaction counts only when the cash changes hands. In accrual accounting, it counts when a transaction is effective. The difference seems insignificant to a casual observer, but to an entrepreneur the results can be as different as night and day. Failing to understand the difference can make or break a business. For example:

Al the shoe store owner agreed to let a customer pay for shoes at a later date. In accrual accounting, the sale is counted once the shoes walk out the door. In cash accounting, there has been no sale yet because no cash has changed hands.

Either way, Al faces the identical problem in terms of his own survival. He paid his supplier to have those shoes in stock. And there is the overhead of salaries, rent, utilities, advertising, etc. He has made a transaction that resulted in no cash coming his way. To top it off, Al must pay taxes on a sale for which he has received nothing.

Part of an Expense Does Not Count

Al's accounting problem gets deeper. The IRS insists that whether Al uses cash or accrual accounting to run his business, he must compute Cost Of Sales (computing the cost of anything for resale) on the accrual basis. The result being that even if Al has spent $15,000 to buy shoes, he can only subtract from his sales the portion of that $15,000 that has actually been delivered to customers, say $5,000. The resulting profit (sales minus expenses) is out of line with the cash it took to generate the sales. He spent $15,000 on shoe inventory, but can deduct only $5,000 because that is all that he delivered to customers.

Money that Has Not Arrived Sometimes Counts

If Al records the sale of shoes on account using cash accounting, the transaction won't count until the cash is received, so Al gets a temporary reprieve. If Al uses accrual accounting, he must count this sale without having received the cash. Let's assume he is on accrual accounting.

Accrual Accounting Lets the Tax Collector Win

Accrual accounting is at the heart of a tax collection strategy to collect more money sooner. If a business can subtract only the inventory sold, as compared to merchandise purchased, the result is more taxes. In Al's case, $15,000 was spent on inventory, of which only $5,000 was delivered to customers. Thus, he can subtract only $5,000 from sales to arrive at net profit. Were Al permitted to subtract the $15,000 he spent, he may have no profit at year's end and, therefore, owe no taxes.

If Al is on accrual accounting, sales count when the customer leaves with the merchandise. Taxes can fall due long before the cash is received from the sale. A delay in customer payment of 30, 60 or 90 days is common.

An additional problem is the need to prepay expenses such as insurance. Al may have to pay $1,200 in annual insurance premiums. In accrual accounting he may only write off the portion which is used, or $100 per month. His cash outlay will exceed his ability to write off the insurance. A year will lapse before he writes off the last $100.

The tax collector imposes hardship upon small business by:
1. Prohibiting the deduction of inventory expenditures from sales until goods are sold.

2. Insisting upon collecting taxes on sales for which payment has not yet been received.

3. Insisting that taxes be paid immediately in cash, impacting the supply of the entrepreneur's most precious resource.

Note: Sole proprietorships, partnerships and corporations must use accrual accounting for the Cost-of-Sales calculation. Each of these entities may elect to use cash accounting to eliminate the payment of taxes on sales which have not been received. Whole Corporations, partnerships with a corporate partner and Sub S corporations with revenue exceeding $5 million dollars must use accrual accounting.

The Hidden Difference Between Cash and Profit

The conventional cash flow statement is too complicated and too expensive for small businesses to generate, yet it is the single most important financial statement a small business can obtain. The *No Entry Accounting*™ fix for this dilemma is the Quick Cash Report, a cash flow statement simple enough for everyone to use.

Conventional accounting methods can generate a cash flow statement, but it is seldom provided by commercial services to small businesses. In the one case in which I have seen it, a small business owner was paying $350 a month for the service. He was spending $4,200 annually for something he did not have the knowledge to use. His accountant tried to explain the statement, but the entrepreneur never understood the accountant's lingo. Had the accounting system been simple enough for the entrepreneur to do on his own, his profit would increase by $4,200 a year for less than one hour of work per month. It is not necessary to know how to perform accounting to this level so long as you understand the implications. To illustrate this level of understanding, consider these two excerpts from the Small Business Total Information System computer programs.

The first report is an income statement showing profit on the cash basis. The center column is for entering corrections for accrual accounting commonly known as accrual adjustments. The third column is an accrual profit and loss statement for the same period year-to-date.

The second report, The Quick Cash Report from *No Entry Accounting*™ exposes the ugly paradox--how conventional statements cause small businesses to fail.

Study the income statement for Apex Products through the first quarter. *(Figure 2.)* Notice that Apex generated a $2,148 profit on a pure cash basis. Pure cash basis means that all cost-of-sale expenses are subtracted as they are paid and not when they are sold. Recording the same data, for the same company, under accrual rules inflates profit by nearly five times to $10,386.

Creating this illusion were some very typical accrual adjustments:
    $5,000 added to sales for accounts receivable.
    $4,500 for inventory not yet sold.
    $720 for insurance not yet used.
    $2,000 for payroll taxes not yet deposited.

The Quick Cash Report

The Quick Cash Report tallies only those items that affect the use of cash, regardless of accounting or tax situations. *(See Figure 3.)* The first thing it shows is that while there was a profit year-to-date, (from the Cash method YTD column) March showed a loss (from the Quick Cash report net profit/loss for March). More important, the year-to-date use of cash, also from the Quick Cash Report, shows a shortfall of $2,090. The owner has spent $2,090 more than operations generated as follows:

Assets: This item is for the cash purchase of, or down payments toward, the purchase of depreciable items. The expense for these items is picked up through

Income Statement				Thru... March 31,	1993	
APEX PRODUCTS						
Sales	Cash YTD	%	Adjustments		Accrual YTD	%
Category A (Deposits)	$30,000	100.00%	$5,000		$35,000	100.00%
Category B						
Returns						
Total Sales	$30,000	100.00%	$5,000		$35,000	100.00%
Cost of Sales						
Category A (Cost of Sales)	$15,000	50.00%	($4,500)		$10,500	30.00%
Category B						
Total Cost of Sales	$15,000	50.00%	($4,500)		$10,500	30.00%
Gross Profit	$15,000	50.00%	$9,500		$24,500	70.00%
Operating Expenses						
Advertising	$300	1.00%			$300	0.86%
Car and Truck						
Commissions						
Depreciation & Sect 179	$300	1.00%			$300	0.86%
Wages	$8,000	26.67%			$8,000	22.86%
Insurance	$1,440	4.80%	($720)		$720	2.06%
Interest on Business Debt	$600	2.00%			$600	1.71%
Legal, Professional						
Office Supplies, Postage						
Rent and Lease						
Repairs and Maintenance						
Supplies Not for Resale						
Taxes and Licenses	$1,500	5.00%			$1,500	4.29%
Travel, Meals and Entertain						
Utilities, Telephone	$250	0.83%			$250	0.71%
Bank Charges						
Office Expense						
User Defined			$2,000		$2,000	5.71%
User Defined						
User Defined						
User Defined						
Business Use of the Home	$463	1.54%			$463	1.32%
Miscellaneous						
Total Operating Expenses	$12,853	42.84%	$1,280		$14,133	40.38%
Net Profit of (Loss)	$2,148	7.16%	$8,220		$10,368	29.62%

Figure 2. The Income Statement produced by the Business Information System reveals the vastly different assessments of a company's health in cash versus accrual accounting systems.

Quick Cash Report	
Assets - Paid in full items only	($2,000)
Net Change in Cash from Liabilities Loans=Cash In, Loan Payments=Cash Out	$200
Draw	($1,200)

Non-Cash Expenses
  Depreciation
  Business Use of the Home
	
	$100
	$154

Capital	
Net Profit/(Loss)	($344)
Cash Shortfall	($3,090)
YTD - Cash Shortfall	($2,090)

Figure 3. The Quick Cash Report generated by the Business Information System is an easily understood version of the cash flow statement, the single most importment financial statement a small business can obtain.

depreciation which may be spread over years and bear no resemblance to the way cash was used to purchase them.

Net Change in Liabilities: Money borrowed does not appear in the income statement, nor does money paid back from earlier loans. Monthly demands to pay down the principal balance of a loan can require significant cash that is not tracked through the income statement.

Draw: The money or equivalent in goods and services removed from the business for personal use. It does not appear on the income statement.

Depreciation and Business Use of the Home: These non-cash expenses are subtracted from Apex's profit, but a check is never written to pay these items. The cash has not left the checking account, and therefore is added back.

Net Profit or Loss: Cash accounting points directly to profit as a source of cash, while loss points directly to a use of cash. Sounds simple, but the impact is dramatic. With accrual accounting there is no such direct access to cash management data.

The cash accounting statement shows a quarter-to-date cash profit of $2,148, while the accrual statement from the same period shows a $10,368 profit. The accounting paradox is exposed when we look at the Quick Cash Report. It shows that the uses of cash in the first quarter have exceeded sources by $2,090. The financial distance between a cash shortfall of $2,090 and a profit of $10,368 is $12,458 (10,368+ to 2,090-). That is more than one third of the year-to-date sales. The problem for the entrepreneur is that neither accrual profit nor pure cash profit generates accurate guidelines by which he may temper the way he uses cash. The small business owner who manages by the Quick Cash Report does not face this danger.

The misinformation that things are going well generated by the accrual statement causes the unsuspecting entrepreneur to spend at the $10,000 level, when in fact he has already spent $2,000 more than he received. The shortfall will only worsen when it comes time to add 3 percent of sales for sales tax, 15.3 percent of profit for self-employment tax, 15 percent profit for federal income tax, and 3 percent of profit for state income tax. The deposits for each will be due within days of the end of the quarter. A Cash Requirements Forecast, another feature of the *Small Business Information System*, will determine how much these items and other unpaid items will add to the cash shortfall in the coming month.

Most of the items contributing data to the Quick Cash Report do not come from the income statement. This is partially why cash data is masked in conventional accounting. Few small business owners are able to read a balance sheet and extract the data necessary for the Quick Cash Report.

An additional factor is conventional statements religiously seek to separate business and personal accounting. This hinders small business owners in managing their cash because business and personal financial matters are extremely difficult to separate. *No Entry Accounting* takes the position that these matters should be combined and has developed a very simple and effective means to deal with the problem.

One departure is to use a single checking account for business and personal spending. Granted, business and personal expenses ultimately need to be separated. The *No Entry* philosophy holds that maintaining separate checking accounts is neither the way nor the point in processing where the separation should take place. The most efficient time to separate business and personal is after the canceled checks have been returned and the checking account is being balanced. At that point, a single handling of business and personal documents will provide the separation mandated by tax requirements. It will simultaneously facilitate the development of a cohesive cash position statement with very little extra effort. *Note: Corporations must separate business and personal accounts per tax law.*

In summary, conventional financial statements and commercial accounting services won't help the small business person succeed. They make the cash management information that is critical to success too hidden, too complicated or too expensive. *No Entry Accounting*™ and *The Small Business Total Information System* provide an easy-to-learn, simple-to-use alternative method.

Chapter Nine

PRICING POLICIES

Many small businesses are in hot water before the grand opening. One culprit is a pricing policy whose impact has not been fully considered. Pricing policies generally fall into three ranges:

- Low markup, high volume sales.
- Medium markup, medium volume sales.
- High markup, low volume sales.

Low Markup, High Volume

The deadliest pricing trap for the new business owner is trying to match the price of the high-volume national chain stores. The markup in these stores is seldom higher than 30 percent. Often it is 10 percent. Chain stores regularly use their volume buying power to offer "loss leaders," commonly purchased items sold at less than cost to lure people into the store. Once in the store, shoppers will wander the well-stocked aisles buying on impulse items with a normal or higher markup. It works. No chain store can get through a weekend without advertising a loss leader.

The impact is greatest upon the entrepreneur when one of these loss leader items happens to be a revenue-producer of the small business. A small business cannot survive on such a low markup. A review of government statistics shows that the gross profit (sales minus the cost of the goods sold) must average at least 60 percent and should be even higher. A small retail operation with sales of $100,000, for example, should have a cost of sales no higher than 40 percent ($40,000) if it hopes to have a chance of reasonable gain. This formula would put the business' pricing markup at 250 percent--$40,000 in goods sold for 2.5 times their cost resulting in $100,000 in sales. The other $60,000 in gross profit can quickly be consumed by the other costs of running a business. To begin with, most business owners would expect a salary of at least $30,000 for the 60-hour weeks they work to run a retail store. That leaves just $30,000 for all other expenses and a return on the capital required to run the business.

At 30 percent markup, gross profit declines dramatically. The same $40,000 worth of goods would have been sold for just $52,000 in revenue. (40,000 x 1.3 = 52,000) This leaves only $12,000 for all other expenses. Not even a wage for the owner would be left.

Let's look at an example of the misuse of this strategy. Roger operated a light aircraft spare parts business out of his basement. It consisted of several hundred commonly used parts. Sales exceeded $100,000 annually, but his markup was strictly wholesale, averaging approximately 30 percent. To develop a customer base, he flew in his company plane to small airports within five states. Each year he showed a small profit, but much of it went into building inventory. Even with no employees or overhead, he was unable to generate a reasonable wage. Bigger competitors with low markup kept his sales volume from reaching a level that would generate a living wage. Roger's family was living off his wife's salary while he pretended to be in business.

This illustrates the problem with the low-markup, high-volume strategy. The small business typically ends up being a low-markup, low-volume operation. High volume requires a large market area, large facilities, and many employees, each of which increases dramatically the sales volume required to make the business work. Only wholesalers, manufacturers, and high-volume retailers can use this method effectively. Some manufacturers rep contracts are essentially low-markup, high-volume businesses as well. They mark up the products they represent by the amount of their commission.

Medium Volume, Medium Price

Most small businesses use a pricing strategy somewhere in the middle. The middle markup is actually the average of various products or services priced to reflect market conditions. In the restaurant business, for example, many markup percentages may be at work.

Wine and beer are priced very competitively at the retail level with a 50 percent markup or less being common. Special brands in upscale operations may be exceptions. Compare that with a dish of homemade custard with butterscotch toping that costs only 10 cents to make but sells for 75 cents. The markup here is 750 percent. Carbonated soft drinks served in a restaurant cost even less per serving and sell for a dollar or more.

Incredibly, steak has one of the lowest markups of meat items in a restaurant. The highest markup is on liver and onions. It can occasionally be purchased for less than 50 cents per pound yet it still fetches the same menu price as many more costly items such as pork chops, sea food, etc.

Unfortunately, items which can be substantially marked up usually are not sold in sufficient volume to make a restaurant viable on their own. Hence, the need for a broad range of items which can generate greater revenue even though it is at a much lower markup. The rule of thumb I used at my restaurant was to mark up each item at least 300 percent unless market conditions would not permit such, as with beer. I could do much better with wine by serving a low-cost choice in a carafe and calling it "the house wine." No item would get on the menu unless it could be reasonably priced at three times the cost of its ingredients. My food cost averaged less than 30 percent because some items--liver and onions, fried chicken and some fish items--could be marked up from five to seven times.

A high markup item loses its value if the chef makes too much and ends up throwing it in the garbage can. So even if your business permits high markup on some items, proper management is still necessary to deliver a reasonable average markup in the end. What at first appears to be a pricing problem, may be a mismanagement problem in disguise.

High Markup, Low Volume

One may read all this and be tempted to think that high markup is the way to go. But there are severe limitations with this pricing strategy. The number of potential clients available for products of this nature may be very limited simply because an item is a luxury few can afford. A perfect gem stone, rare paintings or sculpture are fine products, but not many people are in the market for them. Conversely, clients may be plentiful, but the product is limited. Limited edition stamps, expertly hand-crafted items, or tickets to the Super Bowl are cases in point.

The high-markup low-volume strategy must hinge upon some very limiting factor. However, the strategy need not apply to the entire product line and the chosen product may not be all that special. For example, the custard served in a restaurant permits a very high markup because no one has the time to make it at home, and even with the high markup it is still very affordable.

But to base a business on this pricing strategy, one must have access to a steady stream of merchandise to replace sold items. High markup implies that some limiting factor is at work and so it may be difficult to keep items for sale. It may be that the customer has a special one-time need. A perfect example of a high-markup low-volume business based upon one-time need is Red Adair, the wizard of oil rig fires. He doesn't work every day, but when he does, his special skills command top prices. One sale a month can make a business if the item is a classic automobile. One item a year may be sufficient if you are selling yachts.

But beware. Businesses in the high-markup low-volume arena suffer from the same problems as small businesses. Cash flow is like a roller coaster ride. Cash is drained by the need to purchase a very special item for resale. It may be weeks or months before the item is sold, resulting in a revenue spike which must be managed for an undetermined amount of time until the next sale. The valleys can be treacherous. Large amounts of capital may be tied up in an item or two which cannot be sold at a profit. The key to surviving in a business that uses this strategy may be to stay involved with a regular job or more stable business to help keep the valleys from stretching out. Once established, the entrepreneur can then switch to full time.

What Must You Charge

One way to determine which pricing mechanism is best for your business is to determine the markup required to generate a specific profit. We can begin by collecting data from industry publications available at the public library. It is very difficult to find specific information about a pricing formula itself, but you can compute what it might be. Two publications available at most libraries are the *Statistical Abstract of the United States* and *Annual Statement Studies* published by the Robert Moris Associates. *Annual Statement Studies* details operating expenses by SIC (Standard Industrial Code), which is used by the government for all statistical data involving businesses. Code 5734, for example, is Retailers-Computers and Software. This type of business may have average gross profit of approximately 40 percent. Gross profit equals sales minus the cost of goods for resale. In this case, cost of goods sold would include the cost of the software and computers. Since gross profit is 40 percent, we can compute the average cost of the software and computers sold must be 60 percent of sales.

Next, estimate your expenses including an amount you expect to earn as a salary. The 40 percent left over must cover all your expenses, including taxes, and your profit. Therefore, if you estimate your expenses at $70,000 per year, this $70,000 must equal 40 percent of sales to match the industry average.

$$\frac{\$70{,}000}{40 \text{ percent or } .4} = \$280{,}000$$

How many items must you sell, at several different markups, to achieve $280,000 in sales? You will need to consider competition in your area. The markup needed may not be compatible with the marketplace. If so, you will need to change strategies or perhaps businesses.

Think through your pricing strategy. Be sure that it is compatible with the type of business you hope to have or are already running. It is never too late to change, adapt or modify what may have started out as a great plan and a great idea. Stay flexible by making your goal self employment rather than running a particular type of business. Let your pricing strategy be just as flexible. Capitalize upon the opportunities at hand rather than riding a mistaken or outdated pricing policy into bankruptcy.

Chapter 10

MANAGING CASH FOR TAXES

The central issue in managing cash available for taxes is that the entrepreneur must show more initiative in dealing with the government than with all other vendors. A supplier typically will wait 90 days before requiring an entrepreneur to pay cash on delivery. There would have been several collection attempts before the business was branded "COD." Monthly statements, several phone calls, maybe even a personal visit might be part of the vendor's collection process. The tax collector's timing and technique are quite different.

Many months or years may pass before the "Pay Now" ultimatum strikes. And the financial blow can be delivered repeatedly for a single offense. An example: Things got hectic for Michael around tax time back in 1990. He managed to complete and file his Federal tax return, but ran out of steam before he filed his state income tax. In mid-1993 Michael received a letter from the state tax collector informing him that federal records revealed that the state had not received its fair share. At first, the state was apologetic, suggesting that perhaps they had lost the information. They asked Michael for a copy of his return and documentation supporting the payment of tax. Just in case the error was Michael's, the state had computed the taxes due at $250.

When Michael finally dug up three-year-old records, he came up empty handed--no tax form, no canceled check. He filled in the tax form and a check for $250, thinking the matter was settled. Were the tax man like any other vendor, that would be the case.

A year later Michael received another letter from the state. It indicated that state records showed a penalty and interest due for Michael's 1990 tax. The penalty for not filing a return could equal 75 percent of the delinquent tax plus interest for the period for which the tax had been unpaid. According to the state, Michael owed another $170 for 1990. If Michael didn't pay immediately, it said, there could be more. Grudgingly, Michael once again got out his check book and paid the tax collector.

Let's compare the tax man to another vendor, the banker. Had Michael gone to a banker and borrowed $250 at 10 percent interest, the cost would have been $75. ($25 per year X three years = $75) Consider the effective interest rate with the tax man. It cost Michael $170 to use $250 for three years--approximately 25 percent interest. No business operates very long paying 25 percent interest, even on a very small principal amount.

The Federal tax collectors sometimes take as long to catch a payment problem. Seldom will the IRS alert the entrepreneur to a situation in less than eight months. Yet the interest meter starts running on day one. This puts the responsibility on the small business owners to exercise considerable initiative. You must prevent your business' life blood--cash--from being lost to nonproductive tax penalties and interest and the expense of responding to the inquiries. Know your tax obligation and get it paid on time! Here's some help:

A Little Bookkeeping Goes a Long Way

State and local taxes vary widely, so we will focus on federal and IRS requirements. First, as an entrepreneur you are expected to approximate your tax obligation at year's end. Early in the year, you must estimate annual revenue. Any taxes due need to be deposited by April 15, July 15, Oct. 15 and the following Jan. 15, so January is not too early to begin. This gives you time to save enough cash to meet the anticipated obligation in April.

A good place to start your estimating process is to look at the end of the prior year. Since most small businesses don't even know how they did in the prior year until April when the tax deadline approaches, they are already in trouble for the first quarter of the current year. Most entrepreneurs base their fiscal year on the calendar year. But it can be based on any 12 month period, June through May for example. Regardless of the format, the IRS assumes that a business earns it's income evenly throughout the year. It doesn't factor for peak seasons or weather-related downturns.

Jill projected $40,000 in taxable income after the first year from her food service business. Taxable income is the amount left over after all permissible deductions have been taken. The IRS assumes that $10,000 will be earned each quarter of the year. Therefore, 25 percent of the taxes due on Jill's forecasted $40,000 profit must be deposited at the end of each quarter.

Entrepreneurs like Jill are expected to anticipate earnings as well as the tax bracket those earnings will put her in at yearend. (15 percent anticipated tax bracket X $40,000 taxable income = $6,000 tax due.) Jill will also be responsible for an additional 15.3 percent of her $40,000 profit as self employment tax--FICA, Social Security for self employed persons. This tax is figured on adjusted income, in this case $40,000, before Federal taxes are withheld. Therefore, Jill's total tax obligation will be $12,120. (15 percent of $40,000 for Federal income tax, plus 15.3 percent of $40,000 for Social Security tax) In the absence of other supporting information, Jill is thus expected to deposit $3,040 in April, July, October and the balance by January of the next year.

The Form 2210, a Cash Management Tool

The IRS uses Form 2210 to compute the penalty for late deposit of tax. Few small business people even know of the form or the process it permits. *(See Figures 4 and 5.)* It also serves to document the periods in which your profit was actually earned so that tax deposits can be made in line with income. The form permits the informed small business user to annualize deductions and income based upon four quarters. If your business earns it's profit primarily in the fourth quarter, for example, you may not need to make a deposit in any of the first three quarters when earnings and cash are in short supply.

If the IRS has supplied you the form because it believes you have not made sufficient and timely quarterly deposits, you are instructed to complete the form

Figure 4. IRS Form 2210 is a great tool for determining the cash impact of upcoming tax liabilities.

Form 2210 (1993) — Page 4

Schedule B—Annualized Income Installment Method (see instructions)

Estates and trusts, **do not** use the period ending dates shown to the right. Instead, use the following: 2/28/93, 4/30/93, 7/31/93, and 11/30/93.

		(a) 1/1/93 - 3/31/93	(b) 1/1/93 - 5/31/93	(c) 1/1/93 - 8/31/93	(d) 1/1/93 - 12/31/93
Part I	**Annualized Income Installments** Caution: *Complete lines 20–26 of one column before going to the next column.*				
1	Enter your adjusted gross income for each period (see instructions). (Estates and trusts, enter your taxable income without your exemption for each period.)				
2	Annualization amounts. (Estates and trusts, see instructions.)	4	2.4	1.5	1
3	Annualized income. Multiply line 1 by line 2				
4	Enter your itemized deductions for the period shown in each column. If you do not itemize, enter -0- and skip to line 7. (Estates and trusts, enter -0-, skip to line 9, and enter the amount from line 3 on line 9.)				
5	Annualization amounts	4	2.4	1.5	1
6	Multiply line 4 by line 5 (see instructions if line 3 is more than $54,225)				
7	In each column, enter the full amount of your standard deduction from Form 1040, line 34; or Form 1040A, line 19 (Form 1040NR filers, enter -0-)				
8	Enter line 6 or line 7, whichever is **larger**				
9	Subtract line 8 from line 3				
10	In each column, multiply $2,350 by the total number of exemptions claimed (see instructions if line 3 is more than $81,350). (Estates and trusts, and Form 1040NR filers, enter the exemption amount shown on your tax return.)				
11	Subtract line 10 from line 9				
12	Figure your tax on the amount on line 11 (see instructions)				
13	Form 1040 filers only, enter your self-employment tax from line 40 below				
14	Enter other taxes for each payment period (see instructions)				
15	Total tax. Add lines 12, 13, and 14				
16	For each period, enter the same type of credits as allowed on Form 2210, lines 2, 5, and 6 (see instructions)				
17	Subtract line 16 from line 15. If zero or less, enter -0-				
18	Applicable percentage	22.5%	45%	67.5%	90%
19	Multiply line 17 by line 18				
20	Add the amounts in all preceding columns of line 26	/////			
21	Subtract line 20 from line 19. If zero or less, enter -0-				
22	If you are required to use Schedule A, enter the amounts from Schedule A, line 5, 8, or 19, whichever applies. Otherwise, enter ¼ of line 13, Form 2210, in each column				
23	Enter amount from line 25 of the preceding column of this schedule	/////			
24	Add lines 22 and 23 and enter the total				
25	Subtract line 21 from line 24. If zero or less, enter -0-				/////
26	Enter the **smaller** of line 21 or line 24 here and on Form 2210, line 21 ▶				
Part II	**Annualized Self-Employment Tax**				
27a	Net earnings from self-employment for the period (see instructions)				
b	Annualization amounts	4	2.4	1.5	1
c	Multiply line 27a by line 27b				
28	Social security tax limit	$57,600	$57,600	$57,600	$57,600
29	Enter actual wages subject to social security tax or the 6.2% portion of the 7.65% railroad retirement (tier 1) tax				
30	Annualization amounts	4	2.4	1.5	1
31	Multiply line 29 by line 30				
32	Subtract line 31 from line 28. If zero or less, enter -0-				
33	Multiply the smaller of line 27c or line 32 by .124				
34	Medicare tax limit	$135,000	$135,000	$135,000	$135,000
35	Enter actual wages subject to Medicare tax or the 1.45% portion of the 7.65% railroad retirement (tier 1) tax				
36	Annualization amounts	4	2.4	1.5	1
37	Multiply line 35 by line 36				
38	Subtract line 37 from line 34. If zero or less, enter -0-				
39	Multiply the smaller of line 27c or line 38 by .029				
40	Add lines 33 and 39. Enter the result here and on line 13 above ▶				

Figure 5. The back of IRS Form 2210, a tax form that can be used to determining the cash needed for upcoming tax liabilities.

as documentation for the computation of penalties. The penalty the IRS has computed based upon four even quarters may then be adjusted downward to reflect how profit was actually earned in your business. Jill made no quarterlydeposits for her $40,000 income that first year because she couldn't get to the accounting and had no idea that she would end up owing $12,000 by year's end. Her interest and penalty computed by the IRS was reduced by $1,500 by simply taking time to complete the form which reflected heavy fourth quarter profits.

But Jill was lucky. She was one of the few small business operators who could come up with such a large tax deposit on short notice. She learned to get a copy of the 2210 form (2220 for Corporations) from her local library and use it as a cash management tool rather than a penalty form. She updates the form each quarter to reveal the actual obligation at the end of each deposit period. Thus she is able to make timely deposits, avoid penalties and interest, avoid depositing too much or not enough, and eliminate large year end cash management problems.

Note:<i>The quarterly deposits are made with a set of coupons (1040ES) supplied by the IRS. A coupon for each quarter is mailed in with each deposit check. The instructions for the 1040ES include a place to record the deposits you have made. Even if you do not have the money to send in with your tax filing, significant money can be saved by at least filing on time. One penalty is for not filing. Another is for doing so late--plus interest on the overdue amount.</i>

How to Use the Form

To use the form as a cash management tool see Schedule B--Annualized Income Installment Method. Part 1 helps you compute your income tax obligation. Part 2 helps you compute your Social Security (self-employment) obligation. Note that while the even quarterly deposits are due after the end of months 3, 6, 9, and 12, the annualized deposits are due after months 3, 5, 8, and 12.

Small business who get income statements quarterly, typically get them through months 3, 6, 9, and 12. It gets expensive when the local accountant has to convert the accounting data to the appropriate quarters so it typically does not get done. The accountant will simply send you a notice to deposit one quarter of the estimated tax knowing full well that you have no profit and therefore no cash with which to make the deposit. Later he may charge you extra to complete the form if you do not deposit enough tax in time. You end up either paying too much for accounting or paying penalties to the IRS. You must work to eliminate both.

Begin With Part II

First turn your attention to the second part of the form, which deals with self-employment taxes. Self-Employment Tax is computed on net profit before itemized deductions. The section tests whether your earnings have passed the limits for Social Security and Medicare before the tax is computed. All earnings up to $57,600 are taxable for Social Security. All earnings up to $135,000 are taxable for Medicare. The total is transferred to the taxes portion of Part I. Enter the appropriate total from line 40 of Part II into the suitable columns of Part I.

The four columns require you to enter the *income* for only that period and then multiply it by a number which assumes the same level of earnings for the rest of the year. Quarter one earnings multiplied by four equals annualized earnings at the first quarter rate.

Beginning with line 4, enter the *deductions* expected for the year. A good source for this information would be a prior year 1040 form, Schedule A Itemized Deductions. The annual amount needs to be spread through the dates at the top of columns a,b,c, and d. The total from Part I line 26 is transferred to the 2210 form itself, where any penalty can be computed. The goal is to use the form to compute your obligation and make the deposit on a timely basis.

Once the form is completed it should be submitted with your year-end tax filing as support for anything other than four even quarterly deposits. Granted, this is a hassle. But learning how to use the form can save you big money in penalties and fines. More importantly, it helps to manage cash by not having to make even quarterly deposits when their is simply no requirement to do so or the cash with which to do it.

Watch Out for FICA

FICA is Social Security. It is entirely possible that you may have no income tax liability and still owe thousands of dollars for Social Security. Here's how: William, his wife and three children live in their own home. William started a new business during the year and managed to earn $20,000 as a sole proprietor. But William knew he had plenty of deductions and thought he wouldn't end up owing any tax.

$2,350 Personal exemptions X 5 = $11,750
Property tax on their home = $3,000
Interest on their mortgage = $6,000
Total regular deductions $19,750

William's Adjusted Taxable Income $20,000 - $19,750 in deductions = $250. During the year, William accumulated $2,000 in medical insurance premiums and miscellaneous doctor's office visits. Since $2,000 exceeds 7.5 percent of William's taxable income, he gets to write off the medical expenses as well, leaving him with no taxable income.

But FICA is different. It must be calculated before any deductions are taken. So William is going to have a FICA obligation of ($20,000 X 15 percent = $3,000) $3,000. If $750 was not deposited each quarter or if William did not compute the Annualized Installment Method and make appropriate quarterly deposits other than four even ones, William will be billed for penalties and interest on $3,000 in overdue deposits.

Use the tools available to you and significantly enhance your ability to succeed in business.

Chapter 11

COST CUTTING

Here is the bottom line on business cash management: Run out of cash and you die. While oversimplified here for impact, that statement serves to put cash control on the same level as the survival instinct. Human beings are motivated to live. When faced with the alternative, we instinctively do whatever it takes to stay alive. Business owners must be willing to do the same for their companies.

In the beginning, your business will generate more cost than revenue. That period will eventually be followed by off seasons and economic slumps. To survive, the small business owner must be ever vigilant for opportunities to cut costs and spending. It makes no difference whether the savings stem from personal life or the business environment, since the line between the areas blurs for the small business owner.

Finding ways to *save* money often involves changing the way we think about *spending* money. Keeping our business alive in lean times may depend on us adopting a survivalist mentality--thinking about expenses in ways we otherwise would not when times are good.

Take the Bull by the Horns

One of the greatest cash savers a small business owner can obtain is a good set of tools. This doesn't apply just to men. So many of the gadgets we all use can be repaired very simply if you have the right tool to get the job done. In my 18 years of self employment, there have been several times when I did not know where the next dollar was coming from. Equipment breaks down regardless of whether you are unemployed or making a profit. And it doesn't matter whether the thing needing repair is a personal or business item, they both require cash.

Tradesmen who make repairs sometimes charge an amount high enough that you can afford to make several attempts at the repair yourself, and still spend less than hiring someone to do the job in one try. In the process, you become proficient in handling more and more complex tasks. I entered the trucking business with no mechanical experience other than changing a tire as a teen. I quickly learned that it was not feasible to run a trucking business with that level of mechanical knowledge.

For example, welding costs $30 to $50 dollars an hour. Then there is the downtime of arranging transportation to and from the welding shop and waiting there for service. In a few hours I was taught enough to handle my own welding. The $200 spent for the welder was recouped in a matter of months.

Downtime

Avoiding downtime is one reason new entrepreneurs commonly give for rationalizing purchase of new equipment over less expensive, used equipment which might break down more often. There are two flaws in this thinking: downtime and a flawed operating premise. During the operation of my trucking business, I found that by carrying a set of tools and an inventory of basic parts, I was usually able to get through the busiest days without missing any loads. Major breakdowns, even with used equipment, seldom happen. But minor problems, the kind that take a truck out of revenue-generating service while it is towed, happened frequently.

Towing is very expensive for trucks. The minimum charge was $100 and was often much more. Even under good conditions, a half day would be lost just arranging a tow and getting the truck back home or to a repair facility. The day's revenue was also lost. With a basic set of tools in the truck, I was often able to get the vehicle home under it's own power, where I could perform repair work at night. So my business--designed to earn money at the rate of $45 an hour hauling stone--provided the opportunity to earn the equivalent of $45 an hour doing basic repair work. My salary came from both trucking and mechanical repair, as I would have had to pay $45 an hour for even the most basic kind of repair work. The net effect was to redirect some repair expense back into my own pocket. This not only cuts repair costs at the rate of $45 an hour, but preserves the cash that would otherwise be spent on repairs. Both techniques are vital to the process of effectively managing small business cash.

A Flawed Operating Premise

Much more ominous, however, is the trap of thinking one can operate a business as though it will always be 100 percent operational. Making commitments to always be available is essentially setting up the operational requirement of 100 percent. The cost of trying to operate in such an environment is uncontrollable. For example, many breakdowns occur at the end of the day. If you must be operating the next morning, you are likely to incur overtime charges to keep repair staff working late. It will cost more to rush in parts and to arrange after-hours logistical support.

In the end, the only way to effectively operate in a 100 percent uptime environment is to have duplicates of every machine, support team, and part as well as endless work days so that when something breaks it can be immediately replaced by a spare. The cost of keeping these spares and logistical support is tremendous.

A particularly frightening example are the coast-to-coast truckers who haul fresh produce. When a trucker leaves California with a load of fresh produce, he has committed himself to 100 percent uptime operation. If his truck breaks down en route, he is not only stuck with the cost of repairs, but he may face liability for the produce. It might spoil before he can get his truck towed in, wait for repairs, and complete delivery in New York City. The key is to not lock yourself into contractual commitments that could incur costs beyond what you hope to earn.

The Professionals

Use critical thinking when dealing with professionals. Remember--the professional is simply another small business person trying to make a living. Professionals are using marketing in recent years like never before.

Consider health-related professionals. They now have marketers creating new ways to extract revenue from the average patient. Being insulated from the selling process frees the professionals to do things they ordinarily would not do. "I'm focused on doing the medical work--I've hired someone else to do the selling," says the professional. But the price for that medical work has been driven up by marketing expenses. The result is hidden charges and unnecessary services. An example:

I first noticed the need for glasses when I turned 40. Like so many of us, I believed that the only option was to hop to the optometrist's office, get my eyes examined and pay the piper for some new glasses. The fancy equipment the doctor used on me was impressive. No wonder these exams and glasses cost so much, I thought. The $175 bill for my exam and first pair of glasses was about what I had expected from the advertised specials I had seen. It could have been worse had I chosen the designer frames that were not on sale, or the extras like damage insurance, special tinting and a second pair at half price.

Having considerable experience in the manufacturing environment with computer cost analysis, I was struck by the realization that the manufacture of glasses could benefit dramatically from mass production. A guy could make these lenses by the tens of thousands to various specifications and simply take them out of a drawer as needed. Assembly of a finished pair of glasses could be done by a high school dropout. So why are they so expensive?

Before that question could give me a headache, something else did. After wearing my $175 glasses for a while, I realized that they were causing the headaches I had begun to experience. I couldn't read for more than 20 minutes without having to stop. The lenses turned out to be too powerful and if reading material was not spaced just the right distance from my eyes, the edge of my field of vision became blurred.

It was then that I stumbled upon evidence of the cost savings of mass production in the form of a revolving rack of eyeglasses at an office supply store. The glasses were arranged in order of strength of the lenses. The display included a test pattern so that the customer could try different pairs until the test pattern was crystal clear. The price: $7.99 a pair. Amazing, I thought! Confirmation of my cheap production cost theory was already on the shelf.

The cost-saving magnitude of my hunch really struck home when I came across a bargain bazaar where the rack of glasses was on sale. The price: $1.50 a pair.

They were plastic lenses just like the ones that cost me $175, but were mass produced in China. Now I have pairs scattered in every place I need them. I used to spend hours each week looking for the only pair I owned. I'm saving thousands of dollars a year because I spend more time working and a great deal less time looking for misplaced glasses. I'm saving hundreds of dollars a year more because I would break at least one pair a year. There are fewer costly clerical errors because I can always see better, and my headaches have gone away.

Granted, not everyone can wear glasses off the rack. But many of us can. If you put on a pair of glasses and see just fine, you have given yourself a basic eye exam. Just because the doctor has a whole set of lenses inside an impressive machine doesn't make the process any less dependent upon your judgment as to whether you can see properly. If the rack glasses work, why spend good money for the whole dog and pony show?

A tight cash management position may force us to consider purchases we otherwise would not. Look at auto tires. When our family or company car needs tires, many of us automatically shop for new tires. We know second-hand tires are just as available and cost substantially less. Failing to consider them is illogical when money is tight. Here's why:

A few years ago, I was asked to get a school bus driving license to help get students to athletic competitions. The licensing process requires detailed knowledge of safety features and operating requirements for a school bus. The vehicles are subject to a myriad of regulations and specifications to ensure passenger safety. One set of specifications in particular that struck me concerned the thickness of school bus tires. Front tires must have more rubber than rear tires, so new tires are routinely placed on the front and the old front tires are then moved to the rear. The required minimum tread on a rear tire is just 1/32 of an inch. To the untrained eye of the typical consumer, that tire looks bald.

The typical consumer is like a babe in the woods against a trained tire salesman. "Would you drive your family around with tires like that?" they grimace. "While you are in the shop you might as well get them all changed before you wind up stuck in the boondocks with a flat." Women are especially vulnerable to scare tactics about being alone and stranded. But if 1/32 of an inch is good enough for a school bus full of children, it ought to be good enough for you and me.

A typical set of new tires is more than $200 installed. A premium set can exceed $600. And yet, the "spare tire rack" in stores routinely has tires with 1/4 of an inch or more of tread remaining. New tire warranties typically end when only one quarter of an inch of tread remains. What sounds like a small number is actually 40 to 50 percent of the usable original tire thickness. Therefore, the driver who replaces tires on the advice of the salesman is throwing away nearly half of the original purchase.

The cost adds up quickly if you have a vehicle or two for family use and another one or two for the business. The annual waste in tires can range from $200 to $1,200. The low end figure assumes two vehicles running 50 percent of the tread off $50 tires, the high end is half of expensive tires for four vehicles. Keeping tires properly inflated, aligned and balanced will extend their life and permit use of the whole tire and not just half of it.

Living the Lessons of Cutting Costs

Tough times can teach us cost-cutting lessons that benefit us for the rest of our lives. Ron was forced to cut back because a declining economy had dramatically reduced his business income and activity. Ron spent the extra down time shopping for insurance with a lower premium. He reduced his property taxes by challenging an assessment increase. Library research revealed a quality out-of-state university for his son that cost less than the state university closer to home. Utility costs were reduced by paying better attention to appliance use. When interest rates dropped, Ron refinanced his home loan and cut his mortgage costs by several thousand dollars. Learning to repair broken appliances instead of buying new ones saved thousands of dollars. It cost Ron $2,000 to replace the engine in the family car, but it would have cost more than $10,000 to replace the car. By the end of the year, Ron and his family had reduced regular monthly expenses by nearly $1,500. As the business climate steadily improves, Ron's new lean-and-mean financial position leaves him well positioned to make the most of the business upturn.

You will hear all the taunts..."When are you going to get rid of that 'Sanford and Sons' truck?" "You are so cheap!" Keep in mind that these comments come from people who want you to spend your money their way. Invariably, they lack the understanding of what it takes to make a business succeed. Don't give in. Do what you need to do.

PART FOUR

BATTLES OF THE MIND

Chapter 12

PHYSICAL AND MENTAL ADDICTIONS IN BUSINESS

The basis for my book, *The Small Business Survival Guide*, as well as the *No Entry Accounting System*™, was the belief that most of the eight of 10 businesses that failed in their first five years did so because of poor cash management. I thought that creating a fast, easy way to collect cash management information would help many more entrepreneurs succeed.

Several years and many seminars later, I realized that the simple logic of *No Entry Accounting*™ is often its very shortcoming. That is because the basis for business decisions is so often illogical.

It is clear that where logic and reason end, addiction and/or compulsive behavior begin. Addiction is "to apply habitually." Compulsion is "an irresistible impulse." Take your pick. In either case, one need not look too far to find that some sort of addiction and/or compulsive behavior is behind too many actions of numerous entrepreneurs.

Addictions fall into two basic categories:

Substance Addiction is the inability to control the use of some substance such as alcohol, drugs, nicotine, caffeine or food.

Process Addiction is the inability to deal with social processes on a logical basis. Some common process addictions are workaholism, perfectionism, compulsive need for control, compulsive sexuality, religious fanaticism, thrill seeking, excessive risk taking, etc.

All addictions hurt the operation of a small business. Identifying the addiction at work is often difficult because the individual may regularly substitute one addiction or compulsive behavior for another. A smoker may quit cigarettes only to become a compulsive eater, or an alcoholic may give up drinking only to become a workaholic.

PART ONE...Substance Addiction

We are all familiar with the devastating impact of drug and alcohol addictions on individuals and families. But not all substance addictions are so obvious or commonly known. As a result, the danger they pose to a business is more subtle.

For example, something so seemingly innocuous as caffeine--found in coffee, tea, soda, and chocolate--can be problematic. Caffeine addiction symptoms range from recurring headache and fever to chronic fatigue. A caffeine addict may perspire profusely with a small amount of physical work. The individual can tire quickly and may require an unusual amount of rest. A caffeine addict will develop a host of subtle ways to shift work (particularly physical labor) to others who are more adept at getting the job done. The individual's top priority becomes getting through another day with a paycheck rather than solving a particular work-related problem or providing eight hours of productive work.

Jim was a remodeling contractor and his job frequently required heavy physical labor. On one job, he was required to carry new appliances into a remodeled kitchen. The assistant he had hired helped carry the cook stove in on the first trip. On the second trip, to carry in a dishwasher, Jim began to perspire profusely and grew short of breath. Part way up a flight of stairs, it was necessary for him to stop and rest for several minutes. The appliance was then carried the rest of the way.

At that point, it was again necessary for Jim to rest. To cover his embarrassment at not being able to work at the pace of his assistant, he suggested a 15-minute break. The whole process of carrying both the stove and dishwasher had taken only 15 minutes, and some of that time was at full rest. The assistant didn't require a break, but if the boss suggests it, the assistant will surely take one.

With less than an hour on the job, the crew of two was already taking an unscheduled break. During the break, Jim drank a second can of soda on the job. More caffeine. Jim did not fully recover by the time his can of pop was finished, but he couldn't let on that he was unable to return to work. So he assigned the assistant a menial task and excused himself to make a few telephone calls. Nothing was accomplished by the calls except delaying Jim's return to work.

In the meantime, the assistant had reached a point beyond which he could not proceed without help. Jim assigned still another menial task to be performed while he ran to the store to pick up some fittings that would be required later.

The Resulting Small Business Problems

For Jim's small business, a multitude of problems stem from his unrecognized caffeine addiction. First, Jim was unable to work an eight hour day. On a good day, he accomplished maybe four hours of productive work. If the work was physical, his productive time was closer to two hours. Yet, Jim took a full salary each week from the proceeds of the various jobs.

Secondly, Jim's assistant was only marginally effective because he was not being given direction and was being assigned work which was much more effectively done when working with a partner.

Also, by hiding or perhaps being unaware of his caffeine addiction, Jim spent an inordinate amount of time on breaks. When he called for extra breaks and took the assistant with him, he was essentially doubling his labor cost. He had bid his jobs with ample margin for labor, but was losing money on every job. The problem was marginal labor productivity caused by the countless hours spent dealing with an addiction to caffeine.

Finally, every one of Jim's jobs was well behind schedule. He spent a significant amount of time each day placating customers who wanted their job finished. Eventually, years of taking more out of a business than he had put in had left the company strapped for cash. Jim was in hock up to his ears. Every vendor that had supplied him was vigorously pursuing collection. An irate customer had sued for uncompleted work that had been paid for, and others were about to do the same.

The Shift in the Substance Abused

The pressure of these developments triggered a shift to another substance abuse. One morning Jim showed up late to work. He was listless. His tardy arrival had already cost him. His assistant had been on the clock for an hour and a half with no productivity, waiting for building material Jim was to have brought with him.

Jim helped get the work started and then excused himself to study the blueprint. Moments later, he was asleep in front of the assistant and the customer. Jim's father, a major partner in the business, showed up on the job site. Upon learning that Jim had fallen asleep on the job, he shrugged it off, saying that "Jim let off a little steam last night. He'll be fine once he gets some rest." Jim had gone out drinking, and came home very late and very drunk. The abuse of alcohol had caused him to arrive late to work, keep an employee from working, fall asleep on the job, and embarrass the company in front of a client. By dismissing all this as "letting off a little steam," Jim's father was covering for him and condoning unreasonable and illogical behavior. Jim's father had become what is known as co-dependent. He was supporting illogical, unreasonable behavior so the addict, Jim, would not have to face the difficult process of breaking free of alcohol.

The reason was that both Jim and his father were alcoholics. They had borrowed for several years from prepaid contracts and unpaid vendors to finance their substance addictions. It had finally reached the point where there cumulative debt was more than $100,000 and not a single recent job had resulted in a profit. Entrepreneurship was being used as a cover, a cloak of denial that either had a substance abuse problem.

Alcoholism and the Small Business

Alcohol abuse impacts the small business even when the entrepreneur does not have a drinking problem. Alcoholics are employees and customers, too. Over time, most small businesses will hire an alcoholic or have any number of them for customers. Facing these situations first requires the entrepreneur to understand what constitutes alcoholism. From there, he can deal with the issue in a way that will minimize the financial impact on the small business.

Recognizing Alcoholism

Many surveys and studies have provided slightly different definitions as well as tests for identifying signs of alcoholism. The test below is fairly representative. (The questions were culled from *Children of Alcoholism,* an excellent book on the subject). Answer each question on your own behalf and how you believe an employee or customer would answer based on your experience with them.

> Are you beginning to lie or feel guilty about your drinking?
> Do you turn to alcohol to make yourself feel better?
> Do you make excuses for the reasons you drink?
> Do you gulp your drinks or engage in competitive drinking such as chugging contests?
> Do you drink before parties in order to feel better about going?
> Do you drink to help you sleep?
> Are you annoyed when family or friends talk to you about your drinking?
> Do you drink because you feel tired, depressed, or worried?
> Do you hide your drinking from people with whom you live?
> Do you drink alone?
> Do you occasionally experience blackouts, periods of time you are unable to remember?
> Do you occasionally pass out, or require assistance getting home?
> Do you drink when you are disappointed for consolation?

These types of tests are designed to identify the early signs of alcoholism. A single yes answer indicates the predisposition to a drinking problem. Two yes answers indicate the probability of the disease affecting your life. Three yes answers indicate the need for immediate help and making changes before the disease hits in a very serious way.

How Alcoholism Enters a Business Deal

Gil was gregarious, fun to be with, and was always the life of the party. There were plenty of parties. A week never passed without Gil attending or throwing a party. He was also a free-spirited entrepreneur, a modern-day horse trader. Gil enjoyed boasting about all manner of things he had purchased and sold for large profits.

At one party, Gil told his friend George about a motor home he could buy and easily sell for more than double what the owner wanted for it. The only thing stopping Gil was that he didn't have the $2,000 needed to make the purchase. Anxious to invest in one of Gil's deals, George offered to put up the $2,000. Gil quickly suggested an even split of the proceeds. George would get 50 percent for financing the deal, and Gil would get 50 percent for putting the deal together and selling the motor home.

George wrote a check for $2,000 on the spot. He thought it best to get a note on a piece of scratch paper detailing the 50/50 split and the fact that $2,000 had changed hands. Gil signed it in the presence of his wife and George.

At another party two weeks later, Gil bragged about selling the motor home for $5,000. "That's really great! We each made $1,500 on the deal," exclaimed George. "Have you got a check for me?" Gil laughed and acted as if George was teasing. He walked away to the bar for another drink.

George, too, thought Gil was joking--about not remembering his half of the deal. So he asked again. Gil huffed. "You didn't give me any money for that motor home. Are you crazy?" Gil's voice was very serious.

George produced the note Gil had signed agreeing to split the proceeds. Gil still didn't believe it. It was not until the third witness--Gil's wife--verified the note that Gil grudgingly wrote George a check.

As Gil left for another party he said, "It's a good thing you had that note because there is no way I remember you giving me $2,000."

The Blackout

This is a classic example of an alcoholic blackout. Gil could not remember a single thing about the deal. The shocking thing to George was that during the whole deal Gil didn't even appear drunk. Being an alcoholic, Gil had developed a tolerance to alcohol that let him appear normal even though he had already blacked out. Since Gil routinely made deals while drinking, he had developed a reputation for being an SOB in business deals. Suddenly, there was a logical reason for the reputation.

Don't conduct business while drinking. Even if you feel in control and aware, your customer or employee might not be, even though they appear normal.

The Alcoholic Employee

In *"The Small Business Survival Guide"* I describe what I call the Real Ratio. It is a mathematical ratio which shows how much sales volume is required to recover from a given mistake. For example, a business that is making a 3 percent profit must generate sales of more than 33 times the cost of a mistake just to recoup that loss, with no contribution to profit.

$100 mistake divided by 3 percent net profit:
$100/.03 = $3,333 in sales to recover $100.

Divide $3,333 in sales by the $100 loss - the Real Ratio equals 33:1
That is $33 in sales to recover from each $1.00 mistake.
At 2 percent net profit, the ratio increases to 50:1.

The ratio resulted from my experience with an alcoholic employee. Not having a trained eye to weed out alcoholic employees, I readily hired him for my restaurant. He was likable and good at his job, so I trained him to assist with lockup at night. Giving him the keys to the liquor closet was my big mistake. He promptly began stealing liquor. A monthly inventory uncovered his problem. Most small business owners don't take an inventory, so for many entrepreneurs the loss would have been much greater than the two cases stolen from me. According to the National Restaurant Association, the typical new restaurant earns approximately 2 percent net profit. The Real Ratio, at 50:1 for a 2 percent profit, explains why some businesses never recover from losses caused by an alcoholic employee, especially a longtime one.

Liability Exposure

The alcoholic employee presents special liability insurance problems. They have a significantly higher accident rate on the job. Permitting drinking in the workplace or permitting employees to continue working when they are noticeably under the influence can put you at liability risk for accidents they cause. Don't let employees drink their lunch and return to work. You can't buy enough insurance to protect yourself if they harm someone else or themselves.

White collar drinking is a trickier problem. It is acceptable in business circles to have a drink with lunch or discuss a deal during happy hour. An employee who seems unable to conduct business any other way may not be able to pass the alcoholism test above. The individual may not have a serious problem. But until you can get very close to the individual, you will be unable to judge whether a drinking problem can cause your business trouble.

The Alcoholic Customer

There are many ways an alcoholic customer can knock your business out of business. They commonly require wining and dining to do business in the first place. The dining helps cover the real need, drinking. Even if the wining and dining is affordable, you may face the Gil and George problem of making business deals under the influence.

The alcoholic customer usually prefers company. He will encourage you to match his drinking. He will use any number of tricks (in early cases subconsciously, in advanced cases deliberately) to make you drink as long as he wishes. Funding his drinking habit is often a problem, and keeping you there helps offset the expense. "Don't let the old lady tell you what to do" he may implore. "You've got time for one more, we can sign the papers later." "Come on, you're too stuffy. Let off a little steam." And so forth. The taunts are part of the mechanism alcoholics use to keep company. The effort is to set the stage for the next drink, to misdirect attention from the fact that what the alcoholic really wants is another drink and someone with whom to share it.

The Cost of Alcoholic Clients

Since drinking is expensive, the alcoholic client may be unable to afford your product or service, especially if he, too, is an entrepreneur. Nick and Lou had a masonry business which, from the tone of their stories, was very successful. They were regularly working in the highest-priced neighborhoods. The jobs were all multi-million dollar luxury homes. But there were troubling signs all around. One was their equipment. It was old. Which would be fine if maintained. But their gear was in poor condition. They talked constantly about drunken escapades and where they planned to go after work for a few drinks. Lunch routinely included a beer or two.

The money that went toward a heavy drinking habit left precious little to pay bills at month's end. Nick and Lou put off insolvency by constantly switching stone vendors, even though several were much higher priced. When one cut them off, they would shift to another. The backlog of unpaid vendors grew even though business was booming.

This type of addict never looks far enough ahead to see a downturn coming. So when it finally happens, the booming cash flow that supported the family and the drinking is suddenly insufficient. Maintaining the drinking comes first, then the family, and then, if there is cash left, some of the vendors. Collecting accounts receivable from such businesses is extremely difficult. The supplier will commonly need to pursue collection in the courts. Even if you win in court, there is precious little cash to show for the victory.

Guarding Against Risk

Dealing with an alcoholic may be unavoidable because, especially in the early stages, they are unrecognizable. There are many levels and types of alcoholic. Some only get drunk once a year and then can't find the way home. Some have reached a tolerance level that lets them appear to perform on the job as though nothing was wrong. Others may have two or three beers a day and seem very normal. Alcoholics can be very nice, fun people. They may also have gained a position in their company where you must deal directly with them. So what can you do?

Become knowledgeable enough about alcoholism to recognize its influence in the early stage. Learn to recognize enough of the symptoms so that you do not become entangled in a drinking problem yourself. Libraries are full of books that deal with the problem on any level you chose. Become informed so that you can make intelligent judgments once you find yourself involved with an alcoholic. If you discover the problem in an employee or customer who is valuable to you, comfort them, and assist them in seeking help. Go slowly at first as you are certain to encounter denial, the first line of defense for the alcoholic. Be ready to prove your point with friends and associates. You must not be condescending or display a holier-than-thou attitude. Don't be afraid to get professional help. It is widely available and much of it is free. Alcoholics Anonymous, for example, has chapters everywhere and offers help for alcoholics and the people around them.

When the behavior of a client or employee is either unreasonable or illogical, look for a point from which their behavior is logical. You may see an alcoholic, like Gil, struggling to cover the need for their next drink.

Above all, make it a practice never to conduct business under the influence and let your business associates know that this is the only way you work.

PART TWO...Process Addiction

Process addiction is more subtle and difficult to spot than substance abuse. Much of what is actually process addiction is considered ordinary behavior by the individual. He sees nothing wrong with his thinking. To the people around him, a behavior pattern is seen not as a process addiction, but "just the way he is." One who seeks to make unusual behavior seem ordinary is caught up in process addiction. A major symptom of process addiction is committing or supporting illogical acts even in the face of mountains of evidence against it. Mick and Tanya are a case in point.

Mick had a successful auto body repair business. He and his wife, Tanya, built a comfortable life from the body shop, but were ready to pass on the reins of their enterprise to their married daughter, Jane. Tanya suggested that the son-in-law take over the business. Her objective was to ensure that their daughter benefit from the years of sacrifice that went into building the business. The son-in-law came on board and was taught how to run the business.

Two years later, Mick and Tanya turned up at a *No Entry Accounting*™ seminar. The business was in trouble. The daughter and son-in-law were living high. Mick complained that they had moved from a nice home to a luxurious one. Several new cars had been purchased and traded in for even newer models. Mick had not received the shop rent from the son-in-law for months. The young man had not filed taxes since taking over the business. Mick was on the hook for back taxes and penalties because he still owned the company.

Mick recognized the seriousness of the situation and arranged a private seminar for himself, Tanya, and the son-in-law. We reached the part of the seminar in which each attendee files business documents into the No Entry sort box to generate a tax statement. The documents represented a set of typical transactions for a month within a small business. Tanya rapidly sorted through the documents and began writing on her Schedule C tax form. I had never seen anyone sort the documents so quickly.

It turned out Tanya had used no logic in her sorting. She would simply glance at a document, make an impulsive guess as to where to sort the document, and proceed. Of course, her answers were wrong. As the discussion developed it became clear that Tanya spent money the same way. "If you want it, buy it," was her philosophy. "You should be able to buy what you want." She was an impulsive spender. Her compulsive behavior took the form of making an instant decision without considering the implications later. All that mattered was satisfying a desire, or resolving a conflict, with a snap decision.

This was why Tanya was unfazed by the corrupt handling of the family business by her son-in-law. Her response was: "Our daughter should have the good things in life." If it came from the son-in-law taking all the cash from the business and leaving her and Mick with a large tax liability--so be it. Tanya was an adult living in a fairy tale world. Reason and logic had no place if they went contrary to the life she "should have."

Tanya had passed the problem on to her daughter as well. Jane grew up believing it was up to daddy to provide whatever she wanted. She need not be concerned with how it was provided. That is why, readily, knowingly, she submitted to the robbery of her father's business and her parents' source of retirement income. She felt no shame that her father had no rent income and owed substantial tax while she owned a larger house and drove a more expensive car, with cellular phone to boot.

Recognizing the Problem in Time

A simple technique has served me well in recognizing addiction and compulsive behavior problems. Step back from a conflict or the position one is taking, and look at it from the outside, like someone seeing it for the first time. If what you see is reason and logic, then normal behavior is at work. If an individual has taken a position which seems to be illogical or unreasonable from the perspective of a single involved party, then addiction or compulsive behavior may be at work. When Tanya became aware that no rent was being received from the family business and that a sizable tax liability had been left for Mick, reason and logic dictate that steps must be taken to fix the problem. Her refusal to confront the daughter and son-in-law and order them to live within their means is not reasonable or logical. A year later, nothing had changed. Rent was still not being paid and the tax liability continued to climb.

Mick, after 30 years in business, had finally become co-dependent upon the compulsive behavior of the other three. He could no longer bring himself to do what he knew had to be done. He had to get the son-in-law out of the business and he had to force his wife to take a real-world position in dealing with their daughter. Mick sat idly by as his wife's fairy tale perspective allowed his daughter and son-in-law to milk the family business of it's worth and drive it into debt. Now he is as powerless as the other three to correct the problems. He can no longer maintain reason and logic in the conduct of his financial affairs. Only when the IRS shuts them down, the banks cut them off, and their retirement nest egg is squandered, will the full price of Tanya's addiction and Mick's co-dependency be realized.

Chapter 13

THE BEHAVIORS OF PROCESS ADDICTIONS

Besides the blatant rejection of logic, process addiction can be identified by compulsive behavior. A compulsive process addiction can impact small business in many ways. Workaholism is a compulsive behavior which can sometimes be effectively channeled in a small business. The workaholic uses work to avoid dealing with any number of social or interpersonal relationship problems he may find difficult. If Alice is always busy with work, she need not face the problem that has cropped up in dealing on a personal level with Sue or George. Workaholics are not team players and they will find work even if there is none. But beware, the work is often non-productive "make work."

Workaholics like Alice will frequently work long hours with no extra pay. She will hold out the hours she worked as proof of her company loyalty and imply that those who do not follow her example are not as good an employee as she. Friction results between workaholics and the more balanced individuals to whom a family and life outside interests are important. Sometimes, these more valuable, balanced employees are actually driven away if workaholism becomes the company standard.

To improve Alice's performance then, she needs to be assigned work where she can work independently of associates. She will need constant supervision and direction to keep her efforts from going off on a tangent. At the first sign of a lull, she will make work that may be counterproductive or disruptive to other employees.

Perfectionism is another disorder that may be effectively channeled. Perfectionists can be recognized by their insistence that everything be just so. "If a job is not done right, don't do it at all," they say. In business terms, this may translate to running up the cost of a job with detail and perfection that is not being paid for and that is not required. The perfectionist must be assigned work that requires careful attention to detail, or work with small acceptable tolerance, such as precision machining.

A central issue in process addictions is control. Being in control can be an addiction itself. For these individuals, control is the end rather than the means by which small business problems may be addressed. There are several underlying mechanisms by which the compulsive controller seeks to take and keep charge of the surrounding environment.

Hiding Behind the Business Facade

One way to control a situation is to never allow time to discuss decisions or problems. Mary created such a situation by starting her own business. She was a whirlwind of activity. Since she was the boss, no one could cut her off, or make her attend meetings she didn't wish to attend. Every moment of the day--and night--she had something going. Yet only a small portion of her work was scheduled. The rest she imposed upon herself because she would not trust her employees to handle the simplest task. Another technique involved committing to 10 hours of work when there was only five hours of time available.

When clients tried to talk to Mary on the telephone, she would frequently be talking with someone else simultaneously or typing on her computer during the conversation. As long as she could anticipate the direction of the conversation and her control was not threatened, she would stay on the line. As soon as she felt threatened, however, she would quickly rattle off the long list of things she had to do, the deadlines she had to meet and the people she had to see.

Mary had all her calls screened. If an irate vendor was on the phone inquiring about an overdue bill, for example, she would instruct an employee to take the call and pretend to be too busy. She would stand within earshot, feeding the employee answers she inferred from the employee's end of the conversation. Her voice was clearly audible during these conversations, but she refused to face the caller because she feared she could not control the conversation.

Mary was using her employees as screens through which she could filter situations. As various situations arose, she would only pretend to let employees have the authority they needed to be effective. She withheld the detailed information that they needed so that she could maintain control. It required her to constantly look over their shoulder, rephrasing their questions, feeding them answers and giving them instructions. She was constantly critical of the way her employees handled even unimportant situations. Nothing that she wasn't directly involved with was ever done right.

The Problems Mary Faces

Irate vendors, customers and employees might be tempted to dismiss Mary as a "Boss From Hell." But there are several subtle factors at work in this case:

- Mary was the victim of a process addiction known as workaholism.
- She was supporting her addiction through a process known as triangulation.
- Her inability to trust her employees with even the simplest matters was the mechanism by which she justified her workaholism. If there is so much to do and she is the only one to be trusted to do it, then she can always be in control. No outside influence can enter the whirlwind.
- Secrecy helped maintain the closed circle.
- Constant criticism of employees hints at Mary's perfectionism.
- Her family ultimately paid the price.

Triangulation

Triangulation is a mechanism by which addicts avoid confronting his addiction. It creates distance between the addict and the possibility of having to deal with his addiction. If the sources of confrontation must pass through a third party, the addict maintains control of the flow of information. It is easy to deny input when it does not come directly from a source in a position to argue the matter effectively. Mary used this technique by having her employees answer the phone and conducting telephone conversations through them. She held complete control over what information gets through the filter and, therefore, what she must confront directly. Everyone that dealt with Mary came away dissatisfied, as their needs were seldom met and problems went unsolved. Mary always had the final say because there simply was no time for anything but what she wanted. Through it all, she is in control, twisted though the process may be.

Workaholism

Mary's need for control requires a supporting mechanism. In her case, it was another process addiction--workaholism. The technique of always being busy with work permitted Mary to avoid confronting what she found most difficult--dealing with the people around her on a personal basis. Control is very important to every small business. But making control the end, rather than the means, is a death knell to a small business. No one is ever fully prepared to enter entrepreneurship on his own. To seek control of life by starting one's own business, and then refusing the advice, help, opinions or criticism that can fill in the areas one doesn't know is a surefire ticket to failure.

It may take a few years, and others may be taken in, but the environment Mary created will never succeed. Costs will rise from every facet of business operations. Mary had exceedingly high staff turnover, so she is constantly fighting the front end of a learning curve. She alienated her vendors by refusing to release sufficient information for bills to be processed. A class action lawsuit resulted. Cash flow had grown poor. Vendors have abandoned her. Legal expenses are high because she fights through third parties rather than seek an amicable solution by negotiating directly with problem customers, vendors and employees. Once the balloon of deception gets too large, it simply weakens and bursts.

Lack of Trust

Mary's lack of trust in anyone but herself is an excellent cover for an addictive, compulsive behavior, but it won't make a profit. There are only so many hours in the day and if Mary insists upon doing everything herself, this limited number of hours is not enough. We hear of the effects all the time. "Why didn't you deposit your taxes on time? You would not have all these penalties and the IRS breathing down your back like this." The typical response: "There is never enough time in the day, so I never got to the taxes."

The problem is not time, of course, but an individual's unwillingness to delegate pieces of the work so that it all gets done. If the entrepreneur does not trust anyone to get the pieces done, then the scope of the venture must be limited to the time he can spend on it. Any commitments beyond that will surely fail.

Secrecy as a Means of Control

The control of information has long been a source of considerable power. The more of an operation an individual can keep secret, the greater his power. The company accountant, sometimes called the Controller, is in a position to manipulate an entire operation because of the nature of the information he controls. By selectively releasing and explaining company accounting data, he can influence everything from personnel matters to product design. He can make one department look good and another bad. He can also manipulate company moneys to his own benefit. It can go undetected if his ability to control accounting data becomes paramount in the company.

Only when fellow managers with different perspectives have access to the same data can alternative opinions and ideas be developed. One of the drawbacks of a sole proprietorship is similar. There is no one to view the entrepreneurial landscape from a different perspective and so the sole proprietor is at much greater risk of setting up his own lynching. Starting a business for the opportunity to totally control company information is the wrong reason to become an entrepreneur.

It is healthier to share information with key employees and even customers. It may prevent an owner from making major mistakes. It provides backup in the event of illness or during a vacation. It spreads the workload over several people so that no one person becomes disproportionately important. Employees are more cooperative if they feel trusted and that their input is valued. They make fewer demands when they truly understand that a business may be struggling. They can contribute in a significant way rather than blindly insisting on a top wage and not worrying about how the entrepreneur comes up with the money. The list of pluses goes on. But the secretive manager doesn't care about these considerations. It is being in control which is paramount in his mind.

Perfectionism

That Mary constantly chided her employees for the slightest mistakes indicates that she is a perfectionist. This process addiction develops in an individual who has been criticized endlessly over time. The person comes away feeling that the only way he can be of value to the critical individual, often a parent, is to get everything perfect. If they could only do that, all problems would go away. Naturally, what they experience is one imperfect act after another, leading to a sense of worthlessness. "I can't get anything right," they say. It also leads to the individual becoming overly critical himself. And so the dysfunction passes from one generation to another. At the same time, Mary's criticism of her workers permitted her to more deeply entrench her compulsive need for control. If no one but she can get it right, then she is left to fill her day with more work than she can possibly complete. She can surely maintain control in such an environment.

Tackling the Problem

It can take a lifetime to develop these types of behavior, so there is no quick fix. There are two approaches small business people can take to deal with the problem:

- Get both types of abuser to see that the problem lies with them, rather than those around them.
- Look for ways to turn the process abuser's actions into an asset for the business.

The most common defense mechanism of the addict is to deny the problem. They have innumerable ways of channeling the blame for their actions to those around them. It may be possible to get the abuser to recognize his share of the responsibility. Tanya, for example, may listen to reason if confronted by all the people around and warned that the implications of spending must be explored thoroughly before cash changes hands. She needs to understand that the reckless spending of her son-in-law, even though it may be on behalf of her daughter, can land her in the poor house and her husband in jail for tax fraud. If intervention by friends and family fails, professional help should be sought.

Addiction is Contagious

One way or another, getting help is critical because addiction and compulsive behavior are, in a way, contagious. This can poison the most viable business enterprise. Via the mechanism of co-dependency, people around an addict tend to complement the addictive behavior rather than take a stand and fight it. An addiction is supported in ways the co-dependents often do not recognize or understand. Jim's father had become co-dependent to his son's drinking problem. The telltale sign was when he shrugged off Jim falling asleep on the job as simply "letting off some steam." Inappropriate behavior had become acceptable because it was left unpunished, thereby implying that such behavior is not a serious offense.

The affects of the addiction pass to the co-dependent when that person becomes part of addict's denial system. Jim's father became a co-dependent when he allowed sleeping on the job. The cost to any business accrue rapidly when such behavior becomes a way of doing business.

The Family Ultimately Pays the Price

When the controlling, workaholic entrepreneur starts a business it is his family that pays the price. The more time spent with the business, the less time for the family. Children who grow up in such an environment learn to view the compulsive behavior of the parent as the norm. Through the mechanism of co-dependency, they become part of the problem as they develop a decision-making infrastructure in their young minds. They may develop secretive, workaholic, controlling lifestyles of their own. Perhaps they may develop other addictions.

It is important for each entrepreneur to keep in touch with his original reasons for doing what he does and how he accomplishes it. Is being in business for yourself an end, or is it the means by which you can build a secure financial enterprise? An excellent book for further exploring this subject more is *"The Addictive Organization"* by Anne Wilson Schaef and Diane Fassel.

Chapter 14

DOING BUSINESS WITH THE PROCESS ADDICT

Entrepreneurs must recognize and understand dysfunctional, compulsive and addictive behaviors because daily they face problems produced by these thought patterns. Whether developing a new product or maintaining a successful company, the small business person will be challenged along the way by dysfunctional/compulsive/addictive (DCA) behavior.

Recognizing DCA Behavior

It can be argued that every behavior is logical--even extreme acts such as mass murder--from the perspective of the person committing the act. As a society, we determine DCA behavior by judging an act based on its impact on the human community at large. Widely held social and religious tenets--do not lie, do not steal, do not commit adultery--label behavior as dysfunctional, compulsive or addictive because these acts ultimately cause others to suffer. So the basic standard for recognizing DCA behavior is relatively simple. If an act meets logical and ethical standards, it is considered acceptable. When an individual insists on performing an act that does not meet our group definition of acceptable, it indicates that the logical base from which the act came has been twisted. The logical base is the mind and the collective experience upon which decisions are made. Disease, chemical imbalance, as well as process and substance addictions account for a wide variety of illogical changes to the decision-making base and DCA behaviors.

Analyzing DCA Behavior

To understand why Ned or Agnes lied, stole or committed adultery, we must look at their motivation to act in an unacceptable fashion. Once we understand what drives someone to act a certain way, it is possible to glimpse their logic. The logic behind an individual's dysfunctional behavior becomes apparent if we open ourselves to the same input upon which the person based his decision. Ned lied to his boss--to hide addiction to alcohol. Agnes stole clothes--to cover gambling debts. The key is to grasp dysfunctional logic using our own decision-making mechanism without allowing it to have the same negative impact on us. If we cannot maintain the integrity of our logical base, we enable the behavior or become codependent. We perform Ned's work so that he won't lose his job or help Agnes cover up an illegal act, for example. Accepting illogical motivation does not mean we must support or believe the input. We must accept it to understand the base from which an illogical act seemed logical enough for someone to act upon it.

DCA Behavior in Business

We can understand DCA behavior in the business world with the same technique. If we look at a problem, the position of decision makers or the acts of employees, we can see whether the motivating force is a tenet of logic or addiction. A tenet of addiction is that the addict will deny having a problem despite overwhelming evidence to the contrary. If the addict can successfully convince those around him that everything is fine, his addiction can continue unthreatened. To do so, the addict must deny any input that threatens his image of normalcy.

I once had an employee who came to work so drunk that he could hardly speak and barely stand. When asked if he had been drinking, he very calmly and forthrightly said, "I haven't had a drink in at least two months." His addiction to alcohol was so strong that it cost him all sense of reality. He knew that accepting the input that he was drunk and unable to work would force him to undergo a significant and painful change in his behavior. Namely, he would have to stop drinking. What to others would seem to be an illogical conclusion--that he had nothing to drink for two months--was, in fact, logical to his addicted mind. He must continue to insist that nothing is out of the ordinary so that no change in behavior is required and satisfying his addiction could continue unchecked.

In the business world, process addiction is the most widespread and difficult to overcome. So much so that maintaining gainful, full-time employment in and of itself has become a common process addiction. There is no shortage of stories about people who put their own needs above those of society and fought to preserve an outdated status quo despite mountains of evidence in favor of progress. Some examples are so outlandish that they illustrate, or in time will show, historical significance.

Wright Brothers and Wrong Thinking

Wilbur and Orville Wright are commonly known as the founding fathers of the aviation industry. What is not so widely known is that they very nearly were forced to sell their new technology to another country because of one military officer's illogical compulsion to preserve a network of Washington insiders.

Early aviation was a race to create a working model and compete for development dollars. A competitor to the Wright brothers had a connection to a likely funding source, the U.S. military, through a General in charge of procurement. The General felt compelled to maintain his powerful position by putting himself in control of the emerging aviation industry. He refused to accept, and even withheld, growing evidence that the Wright brothers' airplane design was superior to that of the competitor with whom he was allied. The Wright brothers had overcome the aerodynamic problems caused by wind, but not the compulsive behavior of Washington power brokers. Pressure became so intense that the Wright brothers nearly sold their new technology to a foreign government.

In the end, it was by luck that the Wrights won the U.S. government contract. They knew that the airplane design the U.S. military was on the verge of purchasing would not work in windy conditions. They had experienced the same loss of flight control in windy conditions as the competitor and redesigned their plane. The day of a test flight turned out to be blustery. The Wright brothers were able to take off and fly while the competitor never left the ground, knowing his plane could not be controlled in windy conditions.

One bureaucrat's process addiction could have lead to France, and not the United States, becoming the world leader in aviation. The General who withheld essential data about the Wright brothers was operating under a basic tenet of addiction. He was denying input he knew would force him to alter his position. He had become so addicted to power, and perhaps the possibility of substantial financial gain, that he no longer could act logically and reasonably in the eyes of the general populace. Had his process addiction won his compulsive battle, the U.S. government would have purchased equipment which did not work. (A familiar story.) And a foreign government and it's people would have emerged the beneficiaries of technology created by American citizens.

Cold Fusion and Colder Shoulders

The Wright brothers developed a completely new technology. Boats, trains and trucks simply could not compete and meet the needs that aviation was destined to fulfill. Society had been waiting for such an advancement. Today's new ideas are not that dramatic. Most merely improve existing technology by doing things slightly better or more cheaply. The entrepreneur developing a new product or service faces the same illogical forces as the Wright brothers. The difference today is that the battle begins with the first step to develop the idea, rather than at the end of the process of developing a deliverable package.

A current and ominous example is the plight of chemists Fleischmann and Ponds, who claim to have developed a mechanism the size of a small wastebasket that generates heat from water well in excess of the energy that must be applied. The name used to describe the physics of this process is cold fusion. On a large scale, it would yield unlimited, cheap, clean electrical power--without generating radioactive waste like the widely-used fission process of today's nuclear power plants. When it was identified and publicized five years ago, cold fusion attracted a firestorm of criticism, primarily from physicists involved in government- and industry-funded projects to develop fission as a power source.

These physicists say the experiment results Fleischmann and Ponds are reporting may not be cold fusion. Others say cold fusion is not even possible under generally accepted laws of physics. Therefore, Fleischmann and Ponds must be perpetuating a fraud in the hopes of tapping into government funds.

Fleischmann and Ponds, the Wright brothers of today, have been driven from American shores. Physicists, oil company executives and fellow academics with whom they compete for notoriety and research grants have collectively acted in the predictable manner of a process addict. They have denied the input that such a clean, cheap, power source is even feasible, each fearing that such an awesome possibility might force changes in their beliefs, investments, academic disciplines, and even their jobs.

There is evidence of a status quo process addiction at work. Of all these nay sayers, not one has stepped forward to argue that the heat from the Fleischmann and Pond experiment is not real. Their criticism is that it cannot be cold fusion.

Between you and me, who cares whether the process is cold fusion? Society has a need for a clean energy source and logic dictates that this discovery be thoroughly studied. And it is. But not in this country. The Japanese have recognized that the process involved may be outside the realm of what we can currently explain. Another government has recognized that such tremendous potential must be thoroughly investigated independent of the resistance put up by status quo addicts interested more in protecting their funding, investments and perhaps jobs. By funding the research, the Japanese presumably have locked up a share of the results.

Even Small Business is not Safe

At the small business level, I have experienced these same forces at work. While it isn't on par with the discoveries of flight or fusion, over the past decade my *No Entry Accounting*™ system has received acclaim in national newspapers and magazines, and from seminar students, chambers of commerce and small businesses. There are many methods presently available to accomplish the same ends as *No Entry Accounting*™, but there is substantial evidence that *No Entry Accounting*™ is better at making accounting principles available to people who could not otherwise use them. Yet the colleges that permit the material to be presented as a seminar to small businesses become impenetrable fortresses when it comes to accepting the material as part of regular academic curriculum.

I now recognize that the problem in gaining acceptance from the accounting academic community is not attributable to the validity of the product, but to a widespread process addiction to the status quo. A breakthrough is difficult to advance because there is so much in place to maintain the current system and the supporters who would perpetuate it. Just mention change in the accounting department of any educational institution and no one will even talk to you again. The current system of debits and credits, ledgers and journals, posting, trial balances, etc. will always have value to large businesses and others who earn enough to justify spending thousands of dollars to avoid taxes. This system is supported by a huge academic community addicted to it's entrenchment. While that system delivers for large business, it is woefully inadequate for a much larger number of individuals and small businesses that have a genuine need for the same knowledge without the substantial equity investment conventional accounting demands.

If one accepts these arguments, and substantial evidence exists to support them, then to deny the input is evidence of a status quo process addiction. Addictions are very slow to cure. Left unchallenged by logic, entrenched entities tend to negotiate themselves into a closed loop.

My local teachers union, for example, has negotiated its member's wages to a level at which the school district can only afford to pay salaries by cutting essential programs. Yet teachers maintain that educating children is their top priority. Their actions speak differently. When a strike vote was held, only 15 of the 1,600 teachers voted against a strike. Teachers know that when working parents cannot find babysitters for all the children who can't go to school, the school district will soon give in to salary demands. The educational bureaucracy, in turn, holds taxpayers hostage by listing all the programs that will be cut if taxes aren't raised to meet the teachers' salary demands. The administration is supporting the union's status quo addictive behavior through the mechanism of codependency. As the flow of tax dollars to the school district increases, so do administrative salaries and benefits. Both teachers and administrators as individuals avoid taking blame for selfishly demanding a bigger piece of the pie by blaming the nameless, faceless union.

Common sense shows that, compared to everyone else in the work place, teachers already have a sweet deal. They get four months vacation each year, health insurance and pension benefits, credit unions that provide exceptionally low borrowing rates, and a salary structure run by the teachers themselves. The salary scale includes mandatory wage increases for additional degrees which may benefit no one but the teacher, as well as wages that increase by seniority rather than any definable increase in productivity. Nowhere else in our economy can one find a comparable deal.

The Circle Closes In

Taxpayers in the community were stuck with the tab for the first three teacher strikes, as tax rates soared. Then citizens acted collectively as voters--finally turning out in numbers exceeding the total membership of school district administration and teachers union--to cap property tax increases. As a result, there is no longer a mechanism in place by which an addictive entity such as the teachers union can compulsively demand more money and get it. Co-dependent administrators can no longer use the teachers union to mask their own desires for more income and benefits as the flow of tax dollars increased. Administrators must now fill all new vacancies with persons at the bottom of the salary scale to meet their budget requirements. Many of the discharged teachers would gladly take these entry-level positions but the union will not permit it. In negotiating its contract with the district, the union insisted that new jobs be offered first to laid-off teachers based on seniority rather than qualifications. In one case, an opening for a junior high school science teacher went to a person who had never taught past second grade. Clearly, the teacher was woefully unqualified and the educational needs of students went unmet.

The end result is that a status-quo addicted entity, the union, has secured an inflated wage and benefits package for a dwindling number of process-addicted members. Their process addiction is pushing their own financial interest beyond the community's ability to provide support for a proper education. As programs are cut to control budgets, increasing numbers of veteran teachers must seek much less gainful employment elsewhere.

In the halls of higher education, DCA behavior is even more apparent. It takes the form of tenure, shorter hours than comparably-paid workers in industry, support from a staff of undergraduate assistants who are also on salary, and an array of perks that would make the average man on the street drool. For our nation's young people, it translates to tuition rates that are unaffordable at small colleges. The problem is crippling larger public universities, too. What keeps those institutions going is deeper pockets filled by taxpayers, and a significant numbers of students who would rather have gone to small colleges but couldn't afford it.

Hooray for Bennington College in Vermont! Officials there recently recognized the dysfunctional behavior of the educational elite for what it is--a compulsive grab for more money, more control and less work that has driven thousands of small colleges and universities to the brink of financial ruin. The administration faced the problem by sacking 30 percent of the faculty and abolishing its version of tenure. The result: a 10 percent decrease in tuition. The forecast: look for an increase in enrollment.

None of this will read well to teachers. Process addictions are not easy to see or confront, especially when the status quo under attack is comfortable and familiar. But conventional vision does not always see the real reason behind our actions or those of clients and vendors. Becoming successful as an entrepreneur demands regularly stepping back and separating the reality of people's action from the perception of their potentially flawed thought process.

PART FIVE

BARRIERS OF THOUGHT

Barriers and Battlefields

Chapter 15

THE INFRASTRUCTURE OF DECISION MAKING

Have you ever thought about how you make decisions? How does your mind choose a course of action? Is it drawing upon past experiences to make a conclusion which you are compelled to follow, thereby making you and your mind separate entities? Are your decisions based upon what you were taught by others, perhaps people who didn't even know they were teaching you? How much comes from what you set out to learn versus what you picked up when you had no idea that you were even paying attention?

Surely, your personal decision-making apparatus must consist of good experiences as well as bad ones. Experiences as a Cub Scout or a Brownie, buried deep in your subconscious, may kick in during moments of decision-making. If you have had neither of these experiences, what experiences take their place? In any case, it is very difficult to discern the individual pieces that make up the big, decision-making picture.

A better glimpse of how individuals make decisions is gained by delving into the behavioral sciences. When we do, we find ourselves exploring more deeply different aspects of some of the basic personality types we have identified. Let's look at the decision-making styles of the workaholic, the perfectionist and the compulsive controller.

Decision Making and Workaholism

Andy was foreman for a company that sold cement blocks. He was strong-willed and always ready to take on the world, like many of his employees. Andy came to work early and was always the last one to leave. There were never enough hours in the day to accomplish everything he felt needed to be done. He pushed his workers and regularly demanded overtime hours. If a conflict arose, one could count on Andy to resort to physical threats if things didn't go his way.

Andy's decision-making style was biased toward keeping so busy with work that there was no time for other people or issues. He focused not upon putting in a good day's work, but on filling each waking hour. Work is the behavioral environment in which he feels most comfortable. It cannot argue or present conflicting ideas, and there is always more. Each day must stand on its own in this environment. Fill up today and worry about tomorrow later.

Andy's workaholism influenced the company in many ways. He routinely preferred paying overtime to scheduling the tasks of a particularly busy day to carry over into a light one. He could always rationalize the expenditure--Mrs. Jones needs her material tonight to finish her job by the weekend, we need to get caught up, etc.

The result was the appearance of a loyal and diligent worker, but the cost of payroll soared. Slower days were filled with busy work such as repeatedly cleaning the yard and shifting pallets. The tidy perimeter of the company stretched further into the landscape. The busy work ate up resources. Pallets needed regular restraping from the extra handling and blocks were lost to breakage during the constant reshuffling. Stockpiles of stone and gravel shrank as the mounds were moved from one location to another. Spillage and the discarded "waste" in the bottom of bins was sufficient to consume all the profit. Worst of all, the late evening hours became a cover for pilferage. If Andy had a conflict during the day with his superiors, he felt justified in settling it his way under cover of darkness.

Andy's decisions were not being made with business logic based upon the efficient use of assets to generate a profit. They were based on a behavioral pattern that came with Andy when he was hired. Perhaps he learned his behavior as a child from a parent or other role model who was always buried in work and did not have time for the youngster. If Andy frequently was put off by a compulsive adult who preferred finishing one more job to spending time with the youth, a young mind might conclude that he was often not the most important thing. The subconscious message in such an environment is that work is more important than the individual and must come first.

A behavioral pattern became the foundation for Andy's decision-making processes. Now that Andy is in a decision-making capacity, he unconsciously draws upon his collection of experiences. Since it has always been normal to work all the time, he continually decides upon the choice which permits more work. The need to make a profit, while part of a logical decision-making pattern, was never part of the collective experience upon which he draws when called upon to make a decision. As such, it is not a contributing factor behind his actions.

The Perfectionist Decision Maker

Della was a perfectionist by anyone's standards. Papers had to be retyped over and over until they were perfect. Correction fluid was sacrilege. As a result, lengthy reports took considerable amounts of time and the office atmosphere during such projects was always tense. Della seized control of these projects and would demean anyone who did not share her quest for perfection in spelling and typing. "Don't you even know how to spell?...That phrase should have brackets around it. ...If you can't do it, I'll take care of it myself." The result was that everyone avoided working with her for fear of being made to look foolish. Without staff support, production time soared.

Della's decision-making bias toward perfection meant that form took precedence over function. The perfectionist, like anyone, can only contribute to that portion of a project in which they have expertise. If a perfectionist is permitted to control the whole process, disproportionate emphasis will be given to parts of the project which may be of little consequence. A perfectionist, for example, will put the same effort into an in-house document that no customer will see as he would a company sales brochure which could generate six-figure income.

When the perfectionist is a customer, the problem has a different spin. As they review that brochure, they look for mistakes in spelling or grammar rather than evaluate the overall value of the product or service described. Their decision whether to take a closer look at a new product will depend more on the sales presentation than the products fiscal or logistical merits. If the perfectionist is an employee of a potential client of yours, he may prevent word of the benefits of your product from reaching the right person for the wrong reason.

Because perfection is unreachable, the perfectionist is constantly reminded of what he perceives as his shortcomings. Compliments are spurned because everything could always have been done better. Though perfectly natural, the failure to achieve perfection develops in the perfectionist the belief that achieving perfection would solve all life's problems. Co-workers would finally think highly of them. Family problems could finally be addressed.

Very few business solutions require anything near perfection. Financially expedient compromise must be the standard if one hopes to survive. Marsha bought a computer with a docking station--a slot in which to insert her notebook computer and take advantage of the full-size keyboard and monitor of the workstation. The problem was that the ejection system had malfunctioned. It was supposed to release the notebook computer at the touch of the button. However, the technician who trained Marsha on the system was unfamiliar with this feature, so he inserted the notebook computer as he had learned to insert computer chip cards, as firmly as possible. The rough handling stripped the plastic arm which pushed the computer from the docking station. But it was discovered that with moderate pressure, the computer ran fine and even the partially stripped plastic arm was sufficient to eject the computer from the docking station.

Marsha was furious that her new computer wasn't perfect. She insisted upon a new computer or a full refund. The fact that she could still use the computer to generate business revenue didn't matter. She was prepared to go to court to get her money back, a long and expensive process. She was willing to begin the computer search and purchase cycle all over again--another supplier, another computer system, and a new learning curve. The practical logic of simply getting another plastic part and inserting the computer properly had been lost in a perfectionist's view of how things should be.

Perfection is very expensive. Those few projects which require perfection, such as the space program, are constantly and notoriously over budget. Endless redoing, rescheduling, and retesting consume time and money. But this is the environment in which a perfectionist shines. As long as the extra cost is known from the outset and the end result requires perfection, then everyone benefits. Outside of such situations, rarely can the added costs be recouped at the cash register. Find the right job for your perfectionist employee so that the decisions he makes benefit your business rather than bury it.

Compulsive Control

Linda was a friendly whirlwind of activity, but had to have things her way. Growing up, Linda was never permitted to make her own decisions--not even about her clothing or hair style. Linda was constantly imposed upon to do things she would not have chosen for herself. Her life was one of continual frustration because she could not control her own destiny. That changed when she was promoted to office manager.

Signs went up all around the office reminding workers what needed to be done, when to do it and how to get it done. The copier room was locked up and only Linda had the key. She set herself up as the narrow center of the hourglass. Anything going either way had to go past her--even trivial decisions about the location of decorative plants and how far window blinds should be lowered.

Linda's decision-making bias was developed during the days when every decision that involved her was made by someone else. Now that she was in a decision-making capacity, she seized the opportunity to make up for an entire childhood of decisions she never got to make.

As is the case with other obsessions, the opportunity to make decisions became the end and not the means to build a better business. Her decision to lock the copy room, for example, was supposedly an attempt to reduce the cost of copies. What she was really after, however, was being involved in each decision whether to copy a document. Everyone who wanted to use the copier was now subject to the same review she underwent as a youngster. She finally had control!

The cost will rise in such an environment as staff time is wasted seeking approval for mundane tasks. Pennies saved in paper costs will be more than offset by dollars lost in productivity. When she was out of the office, operations halted. Employee time was wasted because workers could not proceed with an assignment.

Barriers and Battlefields

Making the Really Big Decisions

The move to become self employed is a really big decision. Any of these factors can influence your decision. I have seen many small business operations where the entrepreneur hasn't a moment to spare. They are always busy. Some have turned up in my seminars, where objective number-crunching determined that they were working for two dollars per hour. They cannot accept that all the hours they work would yield so little income. And yet, month after month, there is no profit from 60 and 70 hour weeks.

At any point in running a business, turning your back on the numbers is never the reasonable or logical thing to do. If you ignore the numbers when you launch your effort, chances are you became an entrepreneur for the wrong reason. Your decision must be based upon the reasonable opportunity to make a profit. Do you have to get everything just right? Do you seize every opportunity to deride subordinates if their work is not perfect? Did you start a firm for the opportunity to be totally in control? Does self-employment help cover an insecurity? Are you really in business to be in business?

I have talked with thousands of small business owners over the years. I have noticed that a significant portion of those that fail, or are marginally operating for years under the protective canopy of outside financial support, have something in common--they choose to be in business for reasons which have nothing to do with business logic. This is not to say that they cannot survive. But to improve or grow, it is critical to get in touch with the factors that lead to decisions. It can be the self-knowledge that helps the smalltime entrepreneur finally turn the corner.

Chapter 16

THE COMPETITIVE EDGE IN A PRICING STRATEGY

A basic reckoning point in developing a competitive pricing strategy is the underlying hourly rate that must be achieved to arrive at a given end. It is a given that the hourly rate must include both profit and wage, but leading to that destination are millions of divergent paths. Focusing upon your real needs greatly increases your chances for success.

We can reasonably say that few employees or self-employed entrepreneurs ever earn $80,000 per year. As a practical matter, $80,000 is a very high standard, particularly if the occasional outstanding year is averaged with the three or four years that precede and follow it. At 40 hours per work week for 52 weeks per year, the entrepreneur has 2,080 hours in which to earn his target income. To reach $80,000 one must earn just over $38 per hour.

It seems pretty easy just looking casually at the numbers. Plumbers charge at least $50 per hour in most metropolitan areas. Union construction jobs are routinely bid at $60 per hour. Car dealers charge $54 an hour for a mechanic's services. Accountants and attorneys routinely charge $125 per hour. Even if they don't charge that rate, they often earn it with flat rate fees for work that requires much less time than is apparent. But in the midwestern suburbs where I live (10 towns with a population approaching 400,000), the word is that only an attorney or two earn more than $100,000 a year. Most folks earn well under $50,000, my neighbors say. And I have reason to believe them. So why are pricing and income so far apart?

The Rush to Make Big Money

So few people have ever earned $80,000 per year that there is little understanding of what it takes to earn that much money. The first fallacy is that one can make $80,000 annually by working just 40 hours a week. At the $80,000 level, the standard work week is 60 hours per week with 70-plus hours being quite common.

Let's look at the real wage that an hourly rate generates. Scott, a computer software developer, needed to hire a technical support person to help him produce a database program. The job required a top-notch person who could be relied upon to make professional decisions and perform the work at an advanced, rather than entry, level. He met Anne, a PC Acquisitions Director with a Fortune 500 company. She met all the qualifications required to get the job done. Anne was happy with her $55,000 salary and full-time position. But the job sounded interesting and she agreed to a $40 per hour wage, the maximum Scott said he could afford.

As the pressures of a major project mounted, Anne grew dissatisfied with her hourly rate. She had heard many stories within the data processing community of "consultants" --which she now considered herself--earning $80 to $100 per hour. Even the neighborhood computer store was charging $84 per hour for such mundane jobs as file conversions and on-site training in basic computer concepts. Anne's husband did not work in data processing, but added his two cents. "They're getting $84 per hour at the computer store downtown for that kind of work. Why are you working for a lousy $40 per hour?" Though well under way, the project was far from completion. Scott knew changing his technical support person on such a complex project would set his delivery date back considerably. Production costs could triple.

Reality and Hourly Rates

She and her husband were happy with her full-time position and believed that she was being paid fairly at $55,000 annually. But as is the case with most salaried jobs in today's workplace, a 40 hour work week is rare. The salaried employee is expected to put in the time the job requires. At Anne's job level, 50 hours was the minimum work week. During crunch time, 70 hours was common. Assuming the conservative figure of 50 hours per week, Anne was earning $21 per hour. The $40 per hour Scott was paying Anne was nearly twice the amount that made her and her husband happy. The prospect of instantly doubling Anne's salary would ordinarily be enough incentive for Anne and her husband to pack up and move the family halfway around the world. But in this case, without understanding the numbers behind a salary, doubling Anne's effective rate, in less time, without moving, is not enough to make her husband happy.

Consider too, that Anne's new part-time position carried no operating expenses. My experience has been that to maintain a full-time business of any kind, one must spend approximately half it's cash to keep customers at the door. Sales people, advertising, store hours, showrooms, etc., are expensive. The computer store Anne's husband mentioned, for example, was open retail hours year-round with a full-time staff of 10 people. For much of that time not a single dime was entering the cash register, much less $84 an hour.

Getting the job had not required any marketing investment for Anne. She hadn't even been looking for more work. Nor were there insurance costs. Her full-time job covered the medical expenses and her husband had an insurance plan at his job that they weren't even using. There was no equipment to purchase. Anne had long ago bought a personal computer sufficiently powerful to handle the job Scott was offering. Nor were there physical plant costs. The computer was kept in a room of it's own which was seldom used by the family.

So what appeared to be the same work to Anne's husband was anything but that. The actual programming was certainly the same, but that is where the comparison ends. No one at the computer store was actually earning $84 per hour. Not even close! In fact, the store owner was working for much less that $40 per hour based upon the long hours he had to keep. Plus, he could never get away. Vacation time was nonexistent.

A Genuine Appreciation of the Task at Hand

After looking so closely at the numbers really involved, one can conclude that the $40 per hour rate in this situation is very high. Working part-time and investing nothing, Anne could reach a goal she had never anticipated. With a major project such as Scott's in hand, Anne would be on the brink of launching her own entrepreneurial venture. If Scott's work turned out to be available on a continuing basis, a leisurely search for two or three other customers could lead to a high-income, part-time, home-based business that would free Anne to spend more time with her children, which she wanted. Scott fielded Anne and her husband's objections by pointing out the real value of the hourly wage. The logical base was instrumental in overcoming misconception, resolving the wage dispute and keeping the project on budget.

Highest Price Not Always Biggest Winner

Jack was a plumber trying to build his own business. Like Anne, he wanted it all right away. He knew that the prices he charged on his "side jobs" evenings and weekends were no higher than those of his full-time employer. Jack's business grew to the point at which he bought an advertisement in the local telephone book. Jack had begun to bring his son along on some of these side jobs, training the boy for what Jack was sure would become the family business.

One weekend, Jack and his wife were out of town on vacation. That is when Mr. Jones called with a plumbing emergency. Jones owned a two-flat building with a severely backed up plumbing line that needed to be unplugged. He needed help before Jack was due back. Jack's son had been on this type of emergency call and had heard his father deal with clients on the phone. Jack's son explained that while Jack was unavailable, he was familiar with the work and offered to do the job. Facing the wrath of his tenants, Mr. Jones jumped at the offer. "I can leave right away," the boy said, "but since it is Sunday afternoon the charge will be $150 paid in advance." The boy's dad would have been proud to hear the son negotiate the high rate. Jones didn't like the cash deal, but he was in a predicament.

The boy arrived promptly and in 15 minutes had routed the sewer line the full 100-foot length of his router tool. He told Jones the problem was solved, threw his router in the back of his pickup truck and drove away. Jones informed the tenants that the problem had been fixed and he returned to his own apartment. Five minutes later the phone rang. A furious tenant told him the problem was not gone and now she had another big cleanup job on her hands. Jones immediately reached the boy at the plumbing company and told him to return and take another look at the job. "Well, I don't know what else to do," the boy responded. "You'll have to wait until my father returns."

Now it was Mr. Jones' turn to be furious. "How can you charge $150 for 15 minutes work and not get the job done? What about the sewer line cover you broke and didn't replace?" Again, the answer was, "wait for my dad."

Mr. Jones paid a teen $150 for 15 minutes work--$600 an hour--and he still had the original problem, plus now he needed a new sewer line cover. Jones thought sure that once the father returned he would at least get some of his money back.

Several days later, Jones was able to reach Jack by phone. Jack took the position that the boy had earned the $150 by showing up and routing out the line. The charge was for showing up on a Sunday and was unrelated to any guaranteed result. The broken cover was the result of the age of the fitting, Jack said, and he couldn't accept liability for such things.

Jack used a thought process much like Anne's husband. He had heard that Sunday calls fetch $150 and that is what he charged. It did not matter to him that nothing was accomplished, a part was damaged and not replaced, and there was no overhead for union dues, insurance, wages, or shop maintenance. The result was that Mr. Jones called his local Better Business Bureau and filed a complaint against Jack's plumbing operation. Then he told all his friends of his bad experience. Jack's plumbing business took a big step backward for $150. He didn't realize that $600 per hour demands something a good deal more worthwhile than he provided Mr. Jones.

The Essence of the Competitive Edge

The edge lies in determining what you *need* to arrive at your next level of income. Take it a step at a time. If you are accustomed to working for $15 an hour, it is too much, too soon to ask for $600 per hour, even if you provide a Sunday service most others would not. Remember, it takes at least 50 hours a week for 52 weeks a year to achieve an $80,000 income. Many return customers will be required to reach and maintain that level. If Jack could have earned $30 per hour for himself working on emergency calls on Sundays his name would have spread rapidly. Not only would he be earning more than he could on his regular job, but his customer base would grow rapidly. As your reputation grows, so can your hourly rate. But only enough to reflect your new level of need. Thus you will always retain the competitive edge that will keep customers coming your way.

Chapter 17

THE LOGIC OF BUSINESS

A problem frequently encountered by established small businesses is that the original strategy, if there was one, becomes ineffective. The lack of foresight or the courage to act can hamstring the building of a profitable business. This can take many forms, including these:

The Clerical Log Jam

Years ago, Randy started a business selling auto after-market products such as hand cleaner, spray paint, special engine treatment chemicals, etc. His background was in sales, so it was natural for him to develop a marketing strategy of enticing the customer to buy more. He would devise a new pricing structure with each product he sold and sometimes a different structure for each customer. He felt this gave him the opportunity to close a deal on the spot that he might not otherwise have negotiated if he stuck to a published pricing schedule.

His product line grew along with his sales. But each product was packaged differently. Spray paint came in 12-can cartons. Hand cleaner came in eight-, 12-, and 16-ounce containers. The eight-ounce containers were packaged 12 to the carton, the 12-ounce containers eight to the carton and the 16-ounce containers six to the carton.

To help him close a deal, Randy would improvise discounts on the spot if a prospective client seemed to be on the fence. "Buy 10 cartons of the eight-ounce size and I'll make you a deal. ...Buy two get the third one free. ...Buy one gross of plastic license plate frames and I'll give you 10 packages free." And so it went. After eight years, the inventory had grown to the point at which it was impossible to maintain manually. So, Randy called in a computer company to computerize his inventory and billing.

Lost Logic

The computer consultants began defining the programming problem and quickly became overwhelmed. Nothing Randy was doing followed any programming logic. He worked in no standard unit of measurement. Some items were sold by the gallon, others by the quart or pint. Two pints to the quart, four quarts to the gallon is a base eight numbering system. But other items were sold by the gross and still others by the dozen. These items required a base twelve numbering system. Some items were sold by the pound and others by the ounce. These items required a base 16 numbering system. The computer works with a base 10 numbering system. Working in several different numeric bases complicates the development of a computer program and therefore increases its cost.

Discount Trickery

Randy's practice of discounting made computerizing even more difficult, since none of the discounts had a common base. "Buy two get the third free" is a workable discount method if the free portion has equal value as a percentage over all the items so discounted. That is, if one free case of three equals a 20 percent discount in the eight-ounce size, and one free case of three also equals a 20 percent discount in the 12-ounce size, an automatic computer discount calculation will work. If each different free case results in a different discount percentage, a computer program becomes much more difficult to write. Additional factors about each product line's weight, quantities, and packaging options must be a part of the computer logic. In Randy's case, the options used were so broad that the rule was the exception. The benefits of computerization were significantly diminished because of the large number of exceptions involved, and because of the dramatic cost increase in the computer hardware and software required.

Too Willing to Please

Steve spent years building a trucking business to a staff of five full-time drivers working plenty of overtime. He was putting in long hours, too. The business was built around a single, large customer and the firm's production schedule of shipping parts between various manufacturing operations. The only way Steve could meet demand was to leave an empty trailer at plant A while hauling a loaded unit from A to plant B. The business didn't start that way, but Steve devised this method to stay competitive and keep the contract. Over the years, his trailer fleet grew to the point that each plant had at least one unit waiting to be loaded as production was complete, while another was en route to the next location, where it would wait, until the production schedule permitted, to be unloaded. It was necessary to keep three additional trailers to cover for units unavailable due to repairs, maintenance, safety inspections, etc.

The problem was that Steve did not prepare monthly financial papers, so he never really knew if he had made a profit until the year was over. He had poured hundreds of thousands of dollars into truck tractors, trailers and maintenance and didn't really know anything more than the fact that he was still in business. There were warning signs, though, that Steve failed to heed.

Only Partly in Business

In all his years in business, Steve never obtained a workmen's compensation policy because he didn't have money for the premiums. He was gambling his entire investment and his family's financial welfare that no employee would suffer a serious job-related accident. Despite his considerable investment in equipment and time, he was still not making enough to pay workmen's compensation premiums.

Steve's single, large customer hired a new dispatch chief who was looking to make a name for himself. He brought in a competitor who had cut his price. Steve knew that the competitor could never provide the same level of service, but the new dispatch chief didn't know it. Steve thought the only way to save the client was to cut his own price, but he sought some advice. He was advised to wait it out long enough for the competitor to miss a delivery and feel the pinch of running a seven days a week trucking operation with not enough income to carry the business. In just two weeks, Steve was back. The new carrier had missed critical deliveries, leaving two of the manufacturing plants with an army of employees idled by the lack of parts to meet their production schedule. The former dispatch chief discovered the change and called Steve back. It gave Steve a strong bargaining position to raise his rates to a level that would finally permit him to provide the same basic protection for him and his workers that his large client provided for their workers.

The lesson is that if you give away too much, there is a strong likelihood that it will not be appreciated. Steve's willingness to provide such a high level of service--extra free trailers and free time for loading and unloading--kept him enslaved in a business that was merely buying a job. He was not operating as a business because he could not provide necessary business protection. He continued to take the risks of entrepreneurship with no return. Steve didn't fully understand the contribution his trucking business had made toward the success and profitability of his large client, and so for years he was underpriced.

Unwilling to Go the Distance

Sandy operated an accounting business from her home. She gained clients through networking with friends and neighbors, for whom she provided monthly financial statements and tax preparation. She developed the business over a period of several years to the point where she felt uncomfortable operating from her home. She decided to open an office and furnish it with typical amenities and a new computer system.

Her cost of doing business rose dramatically while the customer base remained the same. She did not know that several customers were considering taking their business in-house by installing their own computer systems while other customers, whose businesses were only marginally successful, were considering shutting their doors. At a time when Sandy needed additional revenue, she was about to experience a dramatic decline in income.

Sandy rented the office in the hope that people would walk in and ask her to do their accounting. That wasn't happening. Sandy sought advice and learned that the way to build an accounting practice is to get out and sell the service. The notion of becoming a sales person to develop--or even save--her accounting practice was frightening. She had always disliked sales people. Too late she learned that the best feature of her home-based accounting business was that customers had sought her or been brought by friends. She did not have to seek out clients and convince them that her particular service was in some way better than the competition.

Sandy realized that the business she had developed into a respectable part-time income working at home was a bird of a different feather when moved up to the next level. Sandy had committed herself to the necessity of growing beyond her comfort level. She had forced upon herself the need to become proficient in a realm from which she had previously remained distant--marketing and sales. As much as she disliked salespeople, Sandy had unknowingly forced herself to become one.

Too often among small business owners are individuals who want the trappings of self-employment but who find it impossible to perform tasks routinely required of small business owners--the expert technician who can fix anything, but is hopelessly overwhelmed by a a tax return; the accountant who can breeze through number crunching, but can't make a sales call; the trucker who can keep rigs on the road and on schedule, but can't make a profit; the salesman who can land a deal but can't track numbers. And so it goes.

The Courage Logic Requires

Small business requires that the entrepreneur be willing and able to handle problems as they arise. There must be a willingness to become meaningfully involved in any aspect of developing a business, no matter how distasteful that aspect may be to the owner. There must always be a critical eye monitoring the gains being made and if there are none, then there must be a willingness to alter the course. To help avoid the kind of traps discussed here, the entrepreneur needs to be looking farther ahead than the next payroll. The entrepreneur needs to have in mind a logical growth pattern that will lead to the success of a business. And he must have the courage to take on whatever task that plan demands.

Barriers and Battlefields

Chapter 18

SEX AND THE SMALL BUSINESS

The last thing a new entrepreneur expects to impact a fledgling enterprise is human sexuality. Only when an entrepreneur becomes entangled in a workplace sexuality issue does the complexity of such problems become known. Even after the situation has destroyed a business--and often a marriage or family as well--the source of the problem remains obscured. Dealing with such complicated, deeply emotional problems, requires an understanding of how people come to act the way they do and of the forces that make up an individual personality.

Sexuality is part of our genetic makeup in the form of a pervasive need to perpetuate the species. Added to this built-in drive are the experiences we have from birth. Many of these experiences stem from early encounters with our own sexuality and that of our care givers. The impact and lessons of these events accumulate, shaping our behavior and the person we become. The experiences collect in our subconscious and serve as the building blocks of our decision-making apparatus. Each time we face a decision or course of action, our collective experience provides the input for the decisions we make. It all happens in a fraction of a second. Is this right? Is this wrong? Should I do it? Should I not? The individualized, subconscious decision-making style combines with the genetic bias to shape the personality through which each of us faces another decision, another social situation, another day. Of all the forces that shape our personality, sexuality is probably the least understood, the least talked about, and potentially the most destructive. How then, do we recognize and address problems that stem from sexuality?

The Hidden Epidemic

For centuries the subject of sexual abuse has been taboo. Only among mental health professionals have the problems stemming from abuse been discussed openly. Occasionally, a person becomes overwhelmed by trying to understand personal problems, seeks professional help and later comes forward to share the experience. It is then that we learn that sexual issues such as incest and child molestation are among our society's most guarded secrets and widespread problems. It is growing more frequent to find men and women who are finally able to share accounts of incest and molestation experiences. Women are usually more willing to talk about early sexual encounters, but now men are coming forward as well. A sex therapist I spoke with acknowledged that "many men" she counsels report forced intercourse with babysitters at a very early age. Others report molestation by their own gender. Understanding and addressing the problems that sexuality can trigger in adult life require clear definitions of early encounters.

Types of Abuse

We are sexual beings from very early in our life. Baby girls can experience clitoral erection just two months after birth. Baby boys experience erections before they are out of diapers. If our body chemistry has armed us with sexuality at this early age, when we understand so little, there is tremendous potential for our sexuality to be shaped and molded before we can even remember the company of another human being.

Incest is sexual abuse at the hands of a primary care giver such as a parent, step parent, or sibling. Molestation is the same abuse carried out by someone other than a primary care giver. Incestuous or molestation experiences become an integral part of the personality and decision-making apparatus without the individual ever knowing how it came to pass.

There are two basic types of incest, overt and covert. In overt incest, there is direct physical contact with the child's genitals. Intercourse is often the physical form of the abuse, but the abuse need not go that far to be considered incest. A common theme in incest is an alcoholic parent. Complicating the crisis, an alcoholic parent may commit incest during alcoholic blackouts and never be aware later of the abuse. The line defining overt incest is clear. Abuse is easily identifiable if physical, genital contact has been made.

Covert incest is much more difficult to identify and address because so much of it appears on the surface to be ordinary behavior. For example, where is the line between acceptable and unacceptable when a man hugs a young girl, perhaps his daughter? Physical contact as a way of expressing affection is socially accepted. Yet the nuances of the message within the contact may be so subtle that only the participants may discern them. Either party may knowingly or unknowingly contribute to the confusion out of ignorance. A child may not be able to recognize the difference between an affectionate hug and one containing sexual implications. Few adults are trained or skilled enough to recognize and then deal with the early expressions of sexuality by children. The adult, however, is responsible for recognizing the difference in hugs and acting appropriately. But the result of confusion is often an unclear message that becomes a long-term part of the personality.

A common breeding ground for covert incest is an environment in which one spouse is not sufficiently available to the other emotionally and sexually. This distance often exists when one or both of the partners is a workaholic, or is involved with some compulsive behavior such as overeating or substance abuse. Self employment provides a convenient cover for an unlimited number of such compulsive behaviors. The affected spouse may seek to satisfy some very basic, perhaps genetic, need for contact with the opposite sex through the child--without physical sexual contact. The result may be a woman who is always "Daddy's Little Girl" or a man who is a "Momma's Boy." If the son or daughter develops a subconscious sexual attachment to the mother or father, which is common, they may have problems later in dealing with sexual peers. They expect intimate relationships to be based upon the experiences developed by growing up with a needy parent. Their sexual decision-making apparatus can consist of experiences that provide sexual intimacy without physical sex. As the affected child grows into adulthood and tries to resolve the conflicts that arise from the difference between their childhood experience and the realities of courtship and marriage, a wide range of problems crop up which few people genuinely understand.

Barriers and Battlefields

How Sexual Problems Manifest in the Workplace

Two real-life examples I have witnessed illustrate how sexual problems can impact a business. They also illustrate the complex nature of sexual issues. No blame should ever be placed on a particular gender or party. In my opinion, the collective problems are like a circle--there is no beginning and no end, and each point in the loop subsequently affects the following points and has been affected by the points preceding it.

John, a middle-age engineer, had been self-employed for a couple years. He had a wife and three children. The kids were doing well. Two had already graduated from college. The wife worked to keep herself busy. They lived in a nice home and took fabulous vacations. Friends would say they had a happy family life.

Business grew to the point where John needed help in the office. He hired Lois, an attractive college graduate about half John's age, to get the company computer system going because the company's clerical work had become burdensome. Through the course of their daily work together, John could not help but notice Lois's behavior. She was much more available than other female employees. At times, he wondered if she was coming on to him. One day, a particularly large deal had finally been won and there was an after-hours celebration party at the office. Under the mantle of drunkenness, an accidental brush with each other in the hallway turned into a passionate embrace. John was now certain that Lois had made herself available and it overwhelmed him. For days, he could scarcely focus on anything else. If a middle-age man could attract a lovely woman just half his age, then he must be more handsome, desirable, and virile than he had imagined. Certainly, more so than his wife of 30 years let him know.

Claiming to have business appointments provided the cover for what became an affair. But events didn't unfold as John had imagined. When the affair reached the point of intimacy, Lois began to act strangely. Her desire to simply be held and caressed was alien to John. Sex, when it finally happened, was an unfulfilling experience for both parties.

What neither of them knew, was that Lois's early experience predisposed her to become involved with a father figure. Sex therapists report that when a young woman prefers to make herself available to a much older man, 80 percent of the time the young woman has been the victim of incest or childhood molestation. Sadly, that same percentage holds true of women who become prostitutes. Lois was never physically abused as a child, but her early experiences left her with a built-in flaw in her decision-making apparatus when it came to relationships.

Lois' mother had little time for her family or husband. She was a horse enthusiast who spent countless hours in the stables. Lois's mom used the heavy workload of caring for as many as 16 horses to avoid intimate contact with her husband. Even evenings and weekends were spent at the barn, so there was little contact between mom and the rest of the family. Lois can scarcely remember her family having a home-cooked meal that she hadn't cooked herself. The family finances suffered as well caring for so many expensive animals. In the process, Lois became daddy's little girl. She played the role of mother with her younger sister and handled the household chores as if she were the woman of the house. She unknowingly filled part of the emotional void felt by a father whose wife was unavailable.

John sought professional help when Lois reacted in ways he didn't understand. He learned that it was not his virility that had attracted the young woman. Rather, Lois was responding to the inappropriate decision-making apparatus that had evolved from her early childhood. She was subconsciously living out a propensity toward father figures in her contact with John.

John's wife noticed a dramatic change in his behavior and demanded an explanation. John realized he had made a big mistake and that his family was the most important thing in his life. He confessed to his wife in the hope of saving his marriage, home and family. It was a very hard time for the family. They made it through, but not without some heavy losses. The episode very nearly ruined the business. The big order that triggered the affair took a back seat as John's escapade unfolded. The order was finally delivered, but there were so many delays and problems that the next contract was awarded to another supplier. The family suffered, too. The children had a difficult time understanding how the father could act as he did. To this day, they probably do not understand the forces at work. Finally, John's relationship with his lifelong partner, his wife, was strained to the limit. Gone were the trust and faith she once had placed in him. A previously successful lifetime relationship had been sacrificed for absolutely no gain. The emotional scars run deep, but over time have been growing less and less visible as some of the trust slowly returns. Most entrepreneurs are not so lucky and never realize how inappropriate sexual behavior ruined their small business.

Sex as Power

Sara was an attractive young woman who developed at an early age and was not emotionally prepared for the attention she received. As a little girl, she noticed the attention she attracted from boys and learned that she could get boys to carry her books and buy her candy or sodas whenever she wanted. In high school, she discovered she could attract and control older and older boys. She didn't realize that the force she was trying to harness was her own sexuality. It was powerful enough to make the opposite sex solve many different problems. If she forgot a book, Joey would get it for her. When she needed a ride somewhere, any number of boys with a car would jump at the opportunity. By the end of her high school years, she had learned to catch the eye of adult men and have them shower her with praise and even thinly-veiled desire. Sara enjoyed the attention she could command.

Years later, Sara was a full-time secretary in a company and did her secretarial work well. She enjoyed being in on top-level meetings where key decisions were made. But soon she wanted more from her job than taking notes and preparing meeting minutes. She wanted to be a manager like the people in the meetings. While Sara was a very good secretary, she had no management skills and little technical knowledge of the company's products. But Sara's early experiences left her with the false impression that her sexuality was an acceptable alternative to traditional ways of acquiring the needed management skills.

Sara turned her attention to Ted, the boss responsible for managerial promotions. In time, it became widely known that she was having an affair with this married man. She pressured him for a promotion and Ted created a new position that only Sara could fill. Sara enjoyed the authority of the position, scheduling meetings for which she had prepared agendas and at which various previously-identified problems would be discussed. As the meetings wore on, accomplishing nothing, it became apparent that simply exercising the authority to call the meetings was the sole purpose of the meetings. Sara did not have the experience to equate power and authority with the responsibility to define a problem and develop a solution.

In meetings, Sara would quickly cut off anyone who asked a difficult question. She would stonewall solutions that she had not developed herself. Finally, two engineers cut to the heart of a technical problem with the effect of destroying her agenda. It became perfectly clear that Sara should not be in charge of the meeting. No one had to say she was incompetent, but everyone present, including Sara, knew it. She stormed out of the meeting, leaving the problem hanging without a solution. She had been using her new authority to satisfy her own need to feel powerful without ever considering that she was threatening the company's prosperity. Her shortcomings as a manager were so glaring that it became a joke around the company.

The problem was that while Sara's affair with Ted was public knowledge, no one had the courage to confront such a high-ranking manager about the delicate issue of putting his mistress in charge of a project for which she was simply not qualified. Finally, the weight of problems caused by the information blockade Sara imposed triggered a major slowdown in product delivery to a large customer. Ted could no longer cover the fact that he had succumbed to sexual manipulation to create a new position which was now threatening the company. His behavior and that of the young woman had needlessly put the company at risk. It cost him his job with the company. It cost the small business owner the considerable investment he had made in training Ted.

Where to Find Help

There are many more examples of sexual behavior creating small business problems. But help is not far away. Counseling is as close as your telephone directory and neighborhood social service agencies. For personal research, the local library is a treasure trove of books that delve as deeply into the subject of sexuality as you care to go. It may even be the largest single section of books in the library. I can suggest two books as a starting point. *The Addictive Organization* by Anne Wilson Schafe and Diane Fassel deals with many forms of compulsive behavior in business. It provides a basis for understanding all sorts of problems we see, but do not recognize in their true form. *Struggle For Intimacy* by Janet G. Woititz covers the types of sexual problems that regularly bring down businesses.

Surely, one does not expect to face sexual issues while making a small business succeed. But just as certain, one will never succeed without dealing with some form of the problem. It may arise from your own psyche, or that of a relative, employee, customer or a vendor. But surely it will arise. Arm yourself with knowledge and insight before the problem blindsides you. Be ready for a long struggle to set things right. It's for sure and it's tough. But a part of being human is our sexual nature.

PART SIX

THE DOCUMENTATION BARRIER

Chapter 19

THE COURTROOM BATTLE AND THE SMALL BUSINESS

The legal system is fraught with traps for the small business person. The biggest is the huge gap between the fair and reasonable delivery of justice and the dollar amounts involved. It begins with the artificially-low small claims court maximum limit of approximately $2,000 and progresses to legal costs that can easily exceed six figures. The only thing to be gained in court by the business person is a sense of vindication. Legal victories become hollow because of the cost of taking a case to court. Bottom line: Winning a case carries no guarantee of receiving your due and if dragged into court, having done nothing wrong offers no protection. We will look at a few basic steps the small business person can take to avoid legal entanglements after examining the lessons in a few case studies. Our first example illustrates the stages of a court proceeding.

Septic and Legal Systems

Eric owned a septic field installation business. He landed a job installing a field in a new residence. It was an unusual system requiring a pump station to move the effluent more than 30 feet to a field which was higher than the pump. As Eric installed the system, he realized that the angle of the buried sewer pipe between the pump and the field would bring the line within 15 inches of the ground surface, a violation of building codes. At that shallow depth, the discharge line was in the frost plane and could freeze. He alerted the contractor, who was also the design engineer. The engineer took the warning as a personal insult and ordered Eric to install the system as drawn and leave designing to him.

Eric did as directed. Three weeks later, the engineer telephoned. The septic system did not pass its review and the inspector ordered the engineer to lower the line. By this time, winter had set in and the ground was frozen solid. Eric reminded the engineer of his earlier warning and told him he would now have to rent a jack hammer to penetrate the frozen ground. Both the jack hammer and the additional hard labor would add significantly to the cost of the job. The engineer cut him short, saying that he had a contract for a price and that Eric had better get the job redone. Eric refused without an agreement for extra money. The engineer hung up in a huff.

Two weeks later, the engineer called again, asking Eric to sign a mechanics lien so that the construction loan could be paid and the sale to the homeowner could be finalized. Eric insisted upon a cashiers check for the money owed him, knowing that once the loan is closed he would have no leverage to obtain payment for the work he had done. The engineer once more hung up in anger.

Two weeks later, Eric drove past the home. To his amazement, the owner had moved in. Eric thought he would have to be paid before the loan could be closed. But the homeowner was already in and Eric had no money to show for his septic installation. The homeowner told Eric that the contractor said there was no outstanding balance on the loan. Eric called the savings and loan association, which told him all subcontractors had signed waivers and been paid. The engineer had forged Eric's signature on a fraudulent wavier.

Enter Small Claims Court

The amount in dispute--$1,350--fell within the state's small claims court limit of $1,500. Eric obtained some legal assistance and completed the forms to file suit against the contractor. It took nearly two months for the case to come to trial. Eric told the judge his side of the story. The contractor told the judge he refused to pay Eric because the job was not finished, and that to get the buyer into the home he filled in the paperwork. The judge ruled in Eric's favor since Eric had warned of the problem and had finished the original installation as designed and directed.

The judge ordered the contractor and Eric to meet in the hallway and negotiate how the money would be paid. A new court date was set, on which Eric would either inform the judge that he had been paid or begin collection proceedings.

Eric's case illustrates the two phases of a court proceeding. The first is determining whose claim has merit. The second is the process of collecting whatever amount the court decides is due the winner. This process can be much more time consuming and complicated. The winner must go through discovery proceedings to determine what assets the loser may have that can be used to settle the claim. If the loser wants to fight, the process can drag on for months until there is nowhere left for the loser to turn. It may also turn out that the loser has no way to pay the amount except in tiny installments spread over years.

Eric was lucky. The new homeowners were still liable for unpaid materials and labor put into their home. Since the contractor had defrauded them by claiming that all liens were satisfied, the contractor was facing a criminal suit if he didn't settle. He did, but Eric was still out several days income from time spent in court and he had to wait a couple months longer to be paid with no finance charges.

Too Big for Small Claims

Our next case illustrates that it can be too expensive to defend ourselves. Neil was a fixer-upper. When he came into some extra cash, he tried to put the money to work by buying an inexpensive rental property and fixing it up. He retained a lawyer to close the purchase of a two-flat in which two families lived. Neil immediately began repairs, starting with a leaky front porch roof. The next morning, he arrived at the two-flat only to discover that the city building department had red tagged his building and was ordering him to stop construction immediately. A visit to city hall revealed two problems. First, Neil had no building permit. That would be easy to fix. But the second problem was far from easy. The city inspector noticed that there were two families living in the building while the neighborhood was zoned for single-family housing.

Neil received a summons to appear in court regarding this zoning violation. He was ordered to convert the two-flat back to a single-family residence and evict the second family. Neil told the judge that he had been lied to by the real estate agent who sold him the property. There were two families in the building when he bought it. He had paid for legal services which he assumed would detect such problems. And now he was losing rent while paying the cost of restoring the building to a single-family residence.

The only help Neil got from the legal system was that the judge agreed that there was substantial evidence of misrepresentation and that Neil should be given several months to iron things out. The judges parting words, "This just goes to show that if you want something to be done right, you have to do it yourself." Neil was stunned by the implication that he was required to oversee the legal work of others to ensure it was done correctly. Clearly, the dollars involved exceeded small claims court limits. Neil discovered that filing a lawsuit would cost a minimum of $10,000. He would have to sue two separate parties, his ex-attorney and the real estate agent. At $120 an hour for legal fees, the going rate in Neil's area, $10,000 would buy only 83 hours of legal work. The cases would have to go uncontested or the 83 hours would likely not be enough time. If either defendant put up a fight or filed a countersuit, legal fees could well exceed $25,000. Neil was overwhelmed. He couldn't understand why the case would take so long. He knew there was no way he could come out ahead dealing with numbers like these. Out of frustration, he simply let the balloon contract expire and let the seller have the building back.

Neil did get some justice. Eight months later, the city contacted him to collect an $800 water bill. It seems that after Neil got out, the tenant moved and left the water running. Neil was happy to inform the city that they would have to pursue the matter with the owners.

The Bigtime Case

Let's return to an earlier case history, that of Tom the trucking contractor. When he started his company, he avoided going deeply into debt financing a new boom truck by buying a used boom and a truck on which it could be mounted. The result was a truck that could perform as well as a new unit at a fraction of the cost.

Tom stayed in the trucking business for quite a few years. He had ridden out a serious recession in the early 1980s. During his years he had plotted his revenue so that he had a good idea of what to expect when another downturn came in 1990. He decided to leave the trucking business rather than suffer through another downturn.

Tom put his equipment up for sale and almost immediately sold the boom truck that had served him well, even though it was 20 years old. More than two years passed. One morning, Tom was served with a lawsuit claiming that he was the owner of a boom truck that was involved in an electrical shock accident two and a half months after it was sold. The new owner had apparently come into contact with a high voltage power line and was seriously injured. The suit was filed days before the statute of limitations was to expire.

Tom had a sinking feeling. He had discontinued the insurance as soon as he sold the truck. That left Tom involved in a lawsuit with the electric company, a wealthy land owner who had rented the building where the accident took place and everyone else the prosecuting attorney could remotely connect with the incident.

The problem here is that some deep pockets are involved in the case. The injured party can sue for a huge amount and settle for a small piece, which is still a big number to me and you. The utility company had a budget for such eventualities, but no one else did. By the time Tom was served, the case had already been in process for two years. Hundreds of hours in legal time had already been expended by the parties and now Tom, the entrepreneur, was pulled into a $150 per hour legal battle that could drag on for years more. There were scores of depositions, in which the parties and witnesses are questioned under oath before the trial. Each deposition seemed to be scheduled, canceled and rescheduled repeatedly.

Tom cleared his first legal hurdle by proving that he had sold the truck and was not the owner. But he still faced a charge that he had manufactured the truck and failed to properly post warnings about using the truck near electrical lines. Tom had purchased the truck in pieces and had several different businesses assemble them. He had not had a direct hand in any of the work. Also, there was an electrical hazard warning sticker posted on the hoist directly in front of the operator at the time of the accident.

None of this mattered. Once sued, Tom's only recourse was to answer the charges with hard evidence in deposition. Tom's attorney hoped to seek a summary judgment which would release him prior to the jury trial. The summary judgment claims that even if the charges are all true, Tom would not be liable anyway. The basis for seeking such a summary judgement was that no reasonable person could offer a guarantee on a 20-year-old truck and no one buying one would expect it. Tom had sold the truck as is, and pointed out each feature on the truck which was not functional at the time of sale. Unfortunately, he could not find the "sold as is" note he was sure he had written. Even having such a "bill of sale" would not have excluded Tom from the suit because he was being sued as the manufacturer as well as the seller.

If Tom had been required to go through a jury trial, his legal bill would surely have reached into the tens of thousands of dollars. He felt it necessary to retain a strong attorney since the parties already involved had a team of high-priced lawyers trying to drag him in on any potential losses.

Tom finally won his summary judgement with the trial still months away. Several new parties had entered the suit, each with the right to depose the parties. Tom got out of the lawsuit before the costly jury trial, but not before his legal bills had soared to $18,000.

Tom's case illustrates the hardest lesson of the legal system--sometimes, there is nothing a reasonable businessman can do to avoid a day in court and paying for it from his own pocket. No bill of sale would have stopped the suit. No reasonable businessman would insure an unused truck for the duration of the statute of limitations. He didn't manufacture the truck and the hazard warning sticker was posted. Sometimes, the innocent are caught under the wheels of justice.

Ways to Limit Your Legal Risks

There are some simple, common sense practices you can follow to protect yourself from being ensnared in the traps of the legal system. Make these practices your standard operating procedure in your business dealings. Doing so cannot guarantee you won't be dragged into the legal arena, but it will certainly reduce your opponent's ammunition.

1. *Obtain appropriate documents.* Many are available from sources other than lawyers. Go to your local office supply store and purchase a copy of every legal document that deals with the type of business transaction with which you are involved. For example, property renters should have a proper lease or rental agreement signed before anyone moves into their building. Do not be afraid to add notes of exclusion and special conditions before the lease is signed. When Sue rented an old house to Mary, it had many things in need of repair. The rent reflected the fact that this was not a premium property. Sue added a clause to her lease that said "repairs requiring less than $25 were the responsibility of the tenant." When Mary twisted her ankle on a broken stair and sued, the case was

immediately dismissed when the cost of the repair was shown to be less than $25. This documentation and a copy of the lease was provided to Sue's insurance company and that was the end of it.

2. *Get it in writing.* Use common sense and don't be in a hurry. Take time to write down your agreements and get signatures. Include notations that would limit your liability. In some states it is simply not permitted to take the position of not being liable. Instead, the small business person needs to be held harmless. That is, you are still liable but the party who might sue you has agreed to hold you harmless should something unforeseen happen. For example, Sid was called upon to install a new pane of glass in a broken window in the middle of a northern winter. Sid explained that carrying a large pane of glass on icy footing was more risk than he could take. He told the customer that he would only take the order if the customer agreed in writing to hold him harmless should someone slip and break the glass. The customer agreed. A worker did slip and the first glass was broken. The customer paid twice. If you are involved in a big deal with many complications, get professional help. But remember that if a job is so complicated and risky that the attorney's bill may overwhelm your profit, do something else.

3. *Do the right thing.* Don't invite trouble by doing something you know is illegal. The classic example is paying employees under the table to avoid paying Social Security, unemployment taxes and workman's compensation premiums. Attorneys have a field day with this entrepreneur. When someone gets injured and you have no workman's compensation insurance, you are inviting the pilferage of your assets by the legal system. That is in addition to the out-of-pocket cost of reconstructive surgery and physical therapy for years to come.

4. *Keep talking.* Instead of fighting, negotiate amicably to arrive at workable agreements. Nobody wins every confrontation. If you try, you will win battles that you really don't want to win. You will become a lone entity which cannot survive without interaction, support and help from others. Work diligently to settle matters before the attorneys add their own bias and monetary needs to your problems. Attorneys have a vested interest in stirring things up rather than delivering quick, amicable solutions. If you are a combative person, don't run a business. Confrontation is everywhere and so are strong-willed customers, employees, and professionals. You will quickly spend much more on attorneys than your small business can generate if you don't accept the occasional loss and move on the wiser.

5. *Use the library.* There are many publications ranging from help with small claims court to preparation of simple legal documents, to complete sets of case histories. Instructions for such things as incorporation, filing for patent, copyright, wills, etc. are there for the asking. Lists of associations are available. You can find one for your industry and obtain information they may provide for simply joining.

6. *Read before signing.* Read agreements that you sign, even if it means hours of dry reading. Be sure that the other party who signs your agreement reads what they are signing. In a health insurance policy, I once discovered an exclusion of my complete cardiovascular system buried on page five. No hint of such an exclusion appeared before that. When I threatened to take the matter to the state insurance board, the exclusion was dropped. Even if you cannot do anything about changing the terms and conditions on a document you must sign, you are still better off knowing exactly what you have given away.

7. *Write win-win pacts.* Make agreements which are good for both sides. One-sided agreements may seem like a big win when they are signed, but they quickly fall apart as the other side realizes you have taken advantage of them. They begin searching for ways to usurp the agreement or perhaps even abandon it. You may gain a dubious reputation. Lopsided agreements seldom work as intended. By the time legal fees are added, you might well come out a big loser.

8. *Network.* Talk with friends and associates who may have some knowledge or experience in matters with which you may be involved. Trade associations you can join often have standard legal forms developed for use within their industry that are free for the asking. Seminars are held by other entrepreneurs whose business it is to sell training. Many of these are free. You may have to sit through a sales pitch, but you can learn a great deal in the process and there is nothing that says you have to buy anything.

9. *Do the leg work.* If the big one comes your way, it seldom happens overnight. You can prepare for it by writing copious notes about pertinent incidents with the time and date. Collect supporting documents so that no expense will be incurred obtaining documents you are sure to require. Remember, if your attorney has to obtain documents, it is at $150 per hour. (Even though it may be his legal assistant who is actually doing the work at $8 per hour.) Find out all you can before the attorneys get involved. Ask for ways in which you may help keep the bill down. Run errands. Order copies of legal documents such as deeds,

liens, etc. yourself because you can do it for a fraction of what attorneys charge. Remember, once the attorneys are involved, everyone is advised to say nothing except in a deposition. That means hour after hour at $150 per.

All of this is contingent upon you being a significant financial target. If you are just starting out, do not own a home and have bills up to your neck, have no fear. You are not worth suing. Everyone else needs to get and keep themselves informed. The inescapable conclusion is that we must all accept adult responsibility in our dynamic world and be held accountable for our actions.

Chapter 20

KEEPING RECORDS

Keeping records is a troublesome, yet mandatory task. What must be kept? How long must various documents be stored? The answer varies, depending upon the document and its purpose. Most people are concerned only with keeping records required by the IRS. But beware! The need for records of even the most innocent transaction, business or personal, can spring up even after decades have passed. Let's look at how the IRS can turn us into "record packrats" and two case studies illustrating why it is a habit worth cultivating.

The IRS--It's Our Party and We'll Pry If We Want To

Every American taxpayer is required to keep records for at least the last three years. The IRS can order you to produce the documents supporting your deductions throughout that period for no other reason than they have chosen to audit your returns. You are on the hook for another three years if the IRS for any reason believes you have understated your income by 25 percent during any of these years.

Their suspicions need not stem from anything you have done illegally. The cause may be an extraneous transaction dumped into your Social Security number. It could result from improper reporting of income or a deduction by your paid tax preparer. Or it could come from a 1099 or W2 a client mailed to the government, but not to you. New, computerized cross-checking techniques available to the IRS might flag your return for an audit for not falling within statistical parameters.

You are fair game forever if you failed to file a return for a year. There is no statute of limitations if you have filed a frivolous return in a tax protest or a fraudulent return containing fake, altered or missing documentation. A recent example is one noted Congressman being ordered to turn over documents dating back nearly 40 years.

What to Bring

If you are called for an audit, you will be required to produce original documents supporting the deductions you have taken. If you said you paid wages of $10,000 back in 1902, you will need canceled checks or properly identifiable paid cash receipts. Proof that you have made appropriate tax deposits such as canceled checks to the IRS or other taxing body, and bank deposit receipts can help support your claim in lieu of original documents. On the other hand, you may be audited because the IRS or other taxing body is not suspicious about the amount of wages that you paid, but that you did not pay any of the tax withheld. Original documents supporting such deposits will be mandatory in this case.

The paper trail generated by computer or other record keeping system is of absolutely no use in an audit except to help you locate the original documents required for the audit. It does not matter who prepared your return. You alone are responsible to the IRS. The paid preparer whose error stuck you with a whopping penalty and back taxes owes you nothing until you prove his negligence. You must take the additional step of suing the preparer for damages, but that is a separate process that does not involve the IRS or delay payment of what you owe. It could take years to recover if it is possible at all.

The Value of Storing Records

Tim and Sally purchased a home 14 years ago. Tim was self-employed and knew that there would be times when there simply was no cash available for making the mortgage payment. Tim decided to make a couple of mortgage payments toward the principal directly from the loan proceeds. He reasoned that if a payment or two were missed, the loan would not go delinquent because the principal would always be paid ahead of the amortization schedule.

Years later, Tim and Sally needed extra cash, so they took out a second mortgage on their home. Tim was still self-employed and had the same income ups and downs. Tim and Sally were granted the loan, and as before they decided to make a two-month prepayment of principal to ensure against the loan going delinquent should they miss a payment or two. The lendor assured them that the new loan was "just like the original" and permitted such payments.

About eight years later, the savings and loan fiasco began to unfold. Sure enough, Tim and Sally's mortgages were held by a savings and loan that failed. The process of finding buyers to pick up the existing mortgages took a couple of years. Tim and Sally received notice that their mortgage was seriously delinquent and that the company which had purchased the rest of the failed thrift's mortgages did not want theirs. Instead, it would be transferred to the Resolution Trust Fund, a government agency for disposing of troubled mortgages. Tim and Sally could lose their home and every dollar paid.

Tim and Sally were shocked by the notice that their loans were delinquent, and not just by a single payment but by thousands of dollars. Tim tried frantically to get a government official to explain how his loan had grown so delinquent without a word of complaint from the savings and loan. His demands won him a full audit. It was handed to him as two computer printouts two inches thick. The bottom lines showed thousands of dollars in delinquencies the Resolution Trust said had accumulated due to late payment penalties. The penalties totaled 14 years for the original loan and nearly eight years for the second mortgage. Tim knew that the savings and loan would never have let such a discrepancy slide for that long, so he compared notes with his passbooks dating back to the original loan dates.

Tim found the problem. The RTC audit never credited the loans with the first two double payments. Tim was sure he had found the evidence that would set the record straight, so he returned to the savings and loan to show the RTC auditor. He was gone! The schedule for RTC auditors was so hectic that he had moved on to the next assignment and could not be reached even through his regional supervisor. Tim took his evidence to the new owners of the savings and loan, where he discovered that one of it's employees had been deeply involved in the audit and perhaps had done it herself. He pointed out that the audit had missed the two prepayments but was instantly rebuffed.

"That must be an error. Nobody ever makes two payments before the loan is ever taken."

"But Miss, this is my passbook that for 14 years has served as the official record of my payments," replied Tim. "You even required copies of these passbooks to proceed with the audit. Why is this information worthless now?"

"There is no record here that can substantiate these payments," she said. "Unless you can come up with canceled checks, the record stands as it is."

The 14-year-old Smoking Gun

Tim was shocked! Could he find an eight-year-old check for the second mortgage, let alone a 14-year-old canceled check on the first loan. For most people, this would have meant the end of the fight and the loss of their home. But Sally and Tim came across both canceled checks in long-forgotten boxes of records. With the new evidence in hand, they returned to the savings and loan confident that the battle could be won and put behind them. The banker, finally, was sympathetic and almost apologetic. But it was too late. The loan had been transferred to the RTC.

A mortgage company had purchased the loan from the RTC, hoping to make a quick profit. They did not want to hear from Tim that the loan was not delinquent and that the RTC had blown the audit. Tim persisted, and after several calls and letters the new mortgage holder appeared to recognize the error, indicating that Tim and Sally needed only continue making the payments.

Three months later, Tim and Sally decided to take advantage of falling interest rates and refinance their mortgage. They were shocked to learn a lien had been placed on the mortgages by the new holder of the paper. It claimed that the balance due was the audited amount less a couple recent payments, a total several thousand dollars higher than Tim knew it should be. When he confronted the new mortgage holder and asked for a statement of account, he discovered that the finance company had added $2,500 to the balance without any notice. Considering all he had been through, learning that the loan company had secretly added $2,500 to his loan balance made Tim furious. He called the mortgage company and used phrases like "fraud" and "truth in lending." The "mistake" was quickly adjusted. Tim and Sally kept their home and secured refinancing because they were able to recover some very old records.

Records as a legal defense

Better recordkeeping could have saved Tom a great deal in legal fees when he was named in a lawsuit in connection with the sale of his old boom truck. His case illustrates the lesson that no transaction documents are too trivial to keep. The suit put him on a search for 10-year-old records.

Tom's first task was to prove that he was not a truck manufacturer. That required records that he had paid others to assemble the boom portion of the truck. He was able to find the original bills for each of the services performed by these various companies and in deposition convinced prosecuting attorneys that he was not a manufacturer.

Another legal hurdle could have been cleared with a simple document--an "as is" bill of sale. Tom was sure he had written such a note at the sale, but could not find it. As a result, Tom was sued for not warning the buyer of the potential hazard when operating a boom truck near power lines. His defense was a document suggested by an attorney for the utility company. The original instruction manual, complete with warnings on the dangers of operating equipment near power lines, was in the glove box of the truck at the time of the accident. Tom remembered showing it to the buyer the day of the sale. Also, the truck was under a power line when it was sold. Tom was certain that he had warned both the buyer and his father, who was operating the truck at the time of the accident, of the electrical hazard. But in the absence of a bill of sale, these claims would have to be made under oath at the deposition.

Tom's attorney found legal precedent that if a person sold such equipment only once and was not engaged in the sale of such items as his business, he could not be held liable for missing or outdated labeling. So, had he gone to trial in the matter, Tom's attorney was certain of victory. But had Tom been able to produce the bill of sale--which indicated "sold as is"--he could have saved himself some of the $18,000 he paid his attorney to find case histories in his defense. And that bill could be dwarfed by the expense of a jury trial.

The moral is to keep everything for as long as you can. You never know when some simple document might protect your life savings. The key is finding an efficient, consistent way to store old records such as the *No Entry Accounting*™ permanent storage box. Had the folks in these true stories used a permanent storage box as these transactions unfolded, they would not have had to depend upon on blind luck to produce old documents to prove their cases. Tom would never have misplaced his "As Is" note and would have found it with the rest of his documentation on the purchase and disposal of business equipment.

PART SEVEN

THE BATTLE FOR GROWTH

Chapter 21

PROMOTING THE SMALL BUSINESS

A promotional advertising campaign is a big gamble for a small business. There are more ways to do it wrong than right, and making a mistake can be fatal. Some key questions:

- How much cash can the business afford to spend on a campaign that may not produce a dime of sales revenue?

- What is the right mix of media? How should the advertising budget be divided between such venues as promotional flyers, newspaper advertisements, radio commercials or yellow pages?

- What is the company's message? That is a deceptively simple question. I've never seen anyone come up with just the right message on the first try. Rather, it is a lengthy process of trial and error. Even paying for expensive professional help carries no guarantee of success.

But there is a way to promote a business that puts no cash at risk and allows the entrepreneur to fine tune his message with each contact. That method is word of mouth.

Developing Word of Mouth Advertising

Richard the carpenter donates his labor and some scrap material to build a Little League outfield fence. As he meets the people associated with Little League baseball, he must be sure to let everyone know that he is available for carpentry work. In exchange for his free labor, Richard's name and telephone number appear on one of the billboards that have become the outfield fence. The result is no-cash advertising plus the opportunity to take his message directly to people who share a common interest, Little League baseball. The fastest, most comfortable way to promote a new business is to begin with people with whom you have something in common. It is the most expedient way to capture the benefits of word of mouth promotion.

Learning from Word of Mouth

As Richard works directly with possible clients, he discovers that each may have a different objection that must be overcome. Mrs. Jones may not have sufficient cash at the moment. Mr. Thompson may place value on the security of dealing with an established contractor. Richard needs to create a list of these objections and develop a plan for dealing with each. For example, he may suggest to Mrs. Jones a way to break a large job into affordable pieces. Mr. Thompson may be swayed by testimonials which speak to the quality and reliability of Richard's work and his ability to complete the job at hand.

Therefore, at the outset, Richard should not be too fussy about the type or size of job he agrees to perform. He should take anything that his tools and skills will reasonably let him perform. The key is not the type of job he has landed, but that he priced his work reasonably, completed the job, performed well and finished on schedule. From these early jobs, he can collect the testimonials needed to move to bigger jobs and greater revenue sources.

Word of Mouth Going Astray

Richard must avoid becoming known for excellent quality at a cheap price, and doing anything to meet even unreasonable customer expectations. In his eagerness to get started, the entrepreneur may easily fall into the trap of generating too high a level of expectations in the eyes of the client. Uninformed buyers, especially, may come to expect perfection at bargain basement prices. Some buyers may even take pleasure in knowing that Richard has hooked himself on a job that should have cost much more than the price quoted. So when Richard ends up working for $2 per hour, it is his own fault.

In such an environment, word of mouth may turn against the small business owner. The stage may be set for expectations which are more likely to generate dissatisfied customers than satisfied customers.

Using Word of Mouth to Identify Prospects

Richard can start developing a list of potential clients while still employed by a contractor. He may be able to establish his own working relationship with people for whom he has worked in the past. Simply letting these people know that he is available after hours and on weekends may be all the promotion he needs to get started. As he moves into full-time self employment, Richard will need to look back and identify the common characteristics of the clientele for whom he has worked. If there is a pattern, it may reveal that he has consistently served a particular market and type of buyer. He may discover a niche which is not served by the competition. Richard can then approach other people in that niche and offer the same type work.

Increasing Word of Mouth

To broaden the effect of word of mouth promotion, try to identify people who regularly meet or hear about the type of client you are seeking. These messengers are in a position to learn of a need for your service in advance of a customer entering the market. Access to such information is extremely valuable. Often, a buyer will deal with the first person who comes along with what they need. Should the prospect shop around, you will still be among the candidates considered.

Participate in functions that offer high visibility at low cost. Local chamber of commerce events, or community activities such as a parade, may get you some attention and let people know you are in business. As you participate in various functions, don't be shy. Let people know what you do for a living. Ask them for the names of people they know who might be looking for your kind of service. Take the time to explain your whole package to good listeners. Explain all the extras you provide which go beyond the industry standard. If you have developed a promotional flyer, give copies to your messenger. Be sure to include information on when and where you can be reached. You may even offer a finder's fee or some free work in exchange for leads that result in a sale.

Build on Success

Once you have completed a job and are happy with your results, make sure your client feels the same way. Ask for their reaction. If the comments are favorable, ask for them in writing even if it is just on scrap paper. Remember, it is not the paper, but the comments that are important. A handwritten note can be retyped. The primary objective is collecting testimonials from satisfied clients. Customers are always willing to share their success stories with the people around them. It could well be that they have a friend or relative who is about to need the same service you have just provided. Be sure to let the happy customer know that you would love the opportunity to do the same good job for their friend or relative.

Keep an ear open for comments like, "My sister mentioned doing something similar next spring." Record them on notes in a prospect file or a calendar so that when spring arrives, you are the first one at the sister's house requesting the opportunity to do her work.

As you perfect the use of word of mouth promotion during the early years with your small business, you may discover it is all you can do to keep up with demand from this effort alone. You may never spend the first dime on advertising and promotion.

Barriers and Battlefields

Chapter 22

THE SALES PORTFOLIO

Testimonials from satisfied customers, whether a handwrittten note on the back of an envelope or a typed letter on corporate stationery, form the beginning of a sales presentation. A testimonial may come in the form of a plaque or award for outstanding service, or an article in a flyer or newspaper. Whatever form they take, collect testimonials so that they can be assembled into the first tool of an effective marketing effort, the sales portfolio.

The portfolio should be filled with product samples, graphic material, photographs, news clippings, testimonial letters--anything that conveys a visual image to your prospect. Your early sales presentations, then, will consist of you and the prospect looking at the same visual material while you narrate. The visual material will cue you as to the next topic to address. The objective is a sales presentation which is hard hitting and to the point. It takes substantial time to put together a really effective portfolio and sales presentation. Let's look at ways to reduce the time and increase your portfolio effectiveness.

Organizing The Sales Presentation

The portfolio must be organized so that the accompanying presentation flows logically. First, establish your credentials. Include copies of any documents which lend credibility to the business you are operating, such as industry honors or awards. Perhaps you were part of a well-recognized project within the community. Include classroom or on-the-job training experience.

Next, document your product or service and how it will meet the needs of your prospective clients. Is it nationally advertised or has it received some special recognition? Is it specially guaranteed or uniquely efficient? Organize your material in a way which allows you to bring your presentation to some strong closing points.

Once you have established yourself and your product, the third part of the portfolio, testimonials and supporting articles, comes into play. This section speaks for your particular ability to deliver the product or service to customers. If the product is of your own creation, testimonials can convince prospects that your product is considered valuable by those who have already spent money for it.

Conclude your presentation with information on pricing, response time, extra services, etc. These items are last because you do not want the prospect to make a decision without having heard the whole story.

Assembling the Pieces

Begin by developing a detailed written outline of the points you wish to raise in each of the areas above. On the subjects of credentials and testimonials, don't be afraid to blow your own horn. No one else will do it for you and listeners aren't offended unless you are lying.

Assemble the pictures, charts, photographs, diagrams, etc. which will serve as the visual portion of the presentation. Each image should serve as a cue for a point you want to make to your prospective customer. The objective is to dovetail the visual material and the written outline. Each picture or testimonial letter should remind you of the next point in the written outline. The result is your prospect will come away with a visual image from your words that will last much longer than words alone.

Place your materials in an attractive binder, notebook or other presentation device. For example, an art student looking for that first job has a large, leather folder that zips shut to safely store a collection of drawings, weaves or prints. An attractive three-ring binder may serve the purpose if it is appropriately covered. The pages should be enclosed in plastic. A product sample may be part of the portfolio.

Develop your sales presentation skills by flipping through the portfolio pages and verbalizing what each image brings to mind. Practice in the mirror as you discuss the sales point you hope to make with each picture chart or graph. The goal is a professionally organized, yet spontaneously delivered, sales presentation. You do not want to leave out anything important, yet you must not sound like the canned pitches of telemarketers and infomercial hosts. The longer the presentation, the more difficult it is to keep the prospect's attention. Keep the presentation as short as possible while still getting the entire message across.

The Top-Notch Portfolio

An extremely important purpose of the portfolio is quickly and effectively handling objections--the reasons people give for not buying your product. Over the course of many sales presentations, accumulate a list of common objections. Look for supporting materials that can be used to help you deal with these common objections. Organize them in the portfolio in such a way that you can shift your presentation to these supporting materials the moment the objection is encountered.

Handle objections immediately! Do not continue your presentation with the thought of coming back to them later. You may forget, or your prospect may believe you are trying to skate around a matter that concerns him. You must effectively address any objections a prospect may have if you hope to get his business. Stay with an objection until you are sure that from the customers' viewpoint you have countered the objection. Only then can you return to your organized presentation.

For example, in selling *No Entry Accounting*™ I frequently hear the objection that accounting is too complicated. Some people think accounting is the exclusive turf of professionals. My portfolio helps me counter this objection with articles and testimonial letters. I have several letters that are textbook examples of how to handle objections. They use the identical words that the prospects use. To top it off, they are handwritten, which lends a sense of credibility and accessibility. Many of those who are frightened by accounting can more easily identify with a handwritten note than a professionally typed letter on business stationery. In the letters, the writers state that having a simplified method of learning gave them the confidence to try--and succeed--at what they thought was reserved for professionals.

Keep any material that might be suitable for the portfolio, but focus on material that is not time sensitive. You will be able to use it for years and save the cost and labor of regularly updating your portfolio. This is especially valuable for products that are not trendy or have a long shelf life.

If someone compliments your work or service, don't be afraid to ask them to jot it down in a note. Remember, the value is in the words people use to describe your work and not what the words may be written upon. Once you have the note, you can dress it up as a typed quotation in your portfolio on nice-looking paper of your choice. Of course, a testimonial written on some nationally recognized letterhead is valuable and you will certainly want to use it. Recognition of your work in the national media works wonders. A national, regional or even local magazine article should be a full page in your portfolio. If such material is in color, be sure that you color copy it for the portfolio.

I have experienced many sales calls in which it was the handwritten note from a very ordinary person that convinced the prospect to buy. I have used many of them effectively in my own portfolio. As you make many presentations, you will develop skill in quickly determining which type of documentation your prospect is likely to prefer.

As you give your presentation, listen attentively to any questions or comments your presentation generates. An initially uninterested prospect will sometimes guide you to what does interest them about what you have to sell--if you only listen closely. Let the prospect guide your presentation. Respond with points you can support with your portfolio. If you have an attentive listener who is letting you run the show, follow the presentation you have developed in the mirror. Don't let your presentation sound repetitive or memorized. You don't want to come across like a train stuck on a single track.

The marketing portfolio pays big dividends even before you become proficient at using it. Once complete, it becomes the syllabus for teaching those who follow you. Your labor can be quickly replicated because your expertise has been captured in print.

Barriers and Battlefields

Chapter 23

SALES--THE FOLLOW UP

The most important ingredient in a sales call is timeliness. Many of the things we small business persons sell are infrequently purchased. That makes it likely that our first contact with a prospective buyer will occur when he is not in the market for one reason or another. When we examine the sales cycle--prospecting, demonstrating, closing, installation or delivery--we see essentially a series of gates through which we must pass to turn our goods and/or services into personal income. If we think of the marketplace as a continuum of opening and closing gates, it puts into perspective the series of events necessary for a sale to materialize and finally become money in our pocket. If we were to label those gates, they would have names like--Too Soon, Too Late, No Cash Now, We're Still Shopping, Afraid to Use Your Product, Too Busy Right Now--and so forth. Only one of these gates is fatal. "Too Late" usually comes from a prospect who has just decided to buy from someone else. Prospects who are on the other side of the rest of these gates, and many similar ones, are worth cataloguing in a follow-up file. Let's look at sales call sins that slam the gates shut and a technique for tracking prospects.

Persistence and Memory

Judy was a self-employed manufacturer's representative who kept an office above a local clothing store where she processed paperwork. She kept weekly office hours, but they were not regular. Phil had a business selling and repairing fax machines. He had heard that Judy was using a fax machine that she purchased when she opened for business three years earlier. He had called upon Judy on several occasions, hoping to demonstrate his new machine, but had been unable to catch her in the office. After several attempts, Phil left Judy a note in hopes that she would call him to arrange the demonstration. The call never came.

Phil was disappointed, of course, because he knew his machine had many worthwhile benefits and he was certain that Judy would agree if only she would take the time to look. Phil's problem was that the window of opportunity to sell Judy a fax machine was simply not open. Many factors could be at work with Judy, but Phil would not be privy to any of them. Judy may find her current fax perfectly adequate. She may be in a cash bind and unable to afford a new machine even if she loved it. She may be on the verge of closing her business. But Phil must be persistent. Only when he hears firsthand from Sue that she has no interest should he give up his quest. The window of opportunity may be on the horizon. Phil can follow up his attempts to speak with Sue via letter. If Sue's current fax is actually three years old, it may need servicing now or in the near future. A letter would fix in Sue's mind Phil's repair service and his new machine. My personal experience has been that when a window of opportunity opens, the last contact and most diligent effort gets the call. You may not be the only vendor competing for the deal, but the chances that you will have your say increase significantly.

The Cost of Failing to Follow Up

Promptly returning telephone messages sounds like simplistic advice. But anyone can fall victim to assuming they know what the call is about and skimping on follow up. Things aren't always what they seem or what we assume they will be. Case in point: Gail ran a real estate business. She was a hard worker with a flair for finding the right home for her customers. She had just completed a sale to the Jones family of a three-bedroom tri-level. The Joneses were very happy with the way the search and purchase had fallen into place. There was a bedroom for their son and daughter and a master bedroom for Mr. and Mrs. Jones. Their little girl had fallen in love with the wallpaper in what was to become her bedroom. The family moved in one weekend and on Monday morning a very disturbed Mr. Jones called Gail. The former owner had removed the wallpaper from the girl's room. "How could someone sell a house and then take the wallpaper with them?" Mr. Jones fumed. "There was nothing in the contract that permitted them to do that," he said.

Gail agreed and apologized for the incident, assuring Mr. Jones that she would talk to the sellers and get back to him. She followed up on the matter, and in two days informed Mr. Jones that the former owner would return and reinstall the wallpaper. Mr. Jones was satisfied. Two weeks passed and the former owners had not complied. Once again, Gail got a telephone call from an irate Mr. Jones. Now the former owners told her that too much of the paper had been ruined by removal and could not be reinstalled. Gail knew Mr. Jones would be furious and convinced the former owners to forward a check for the cost of the paper and a small installation fee. The matter was resolved.

Now it was Mrs. Jones turn to make irate calls to Gail. Mrs. Jones noticed that several small pine trees that had been on the grounds when the house was up for sale were now gone. She was certain that the former owner had dug up and taken the trees when they moved. Gail had never heard of a seller doing such a thing, and contacted the former owners. She demanded enough money to replace the trees and threatened legal action. She got the money immediately, purchased new trees and delivered them to the Joneses.

It was only 12 months later when Gail got a telephone message with Mr. Jones' name on it. When she did not call after two days, Mr. Jones tried again. He asked the secretary if Gail had received the first message and was told she had. Still, there was no call from Gail. It turned out Mr. Jones had been promoted and had to move again. He had been calling to list his house for sale with Gail because he liked her followup in handling his messy purchase. He wanted to reward her with the listing of his new home. But he had to report to his new office in 30 days and the home had to be listed right away. Since Gail wouldn't call back, he called another agent who arrived at the house within the hour. The papers were signed immediately.

The Cardinal Sin of Selling

Gail had committed the cardinal sin in selling. She went to the wall for a prospective customer and at the critical moment failed to follow up. She had put in the work to earn her next listing commission by helping the Joneses through a really mixed up real estate transaction. She did all this when they weren't her customers. The seller was paying her commission. Because she assumed that some other problem had cropped up, she avoided returning the phone call. She failed to put thousands of dollars in her pocket because she ignored basic telephone etiquette.

Keeping Priorities in Order

After three years, Charley's construction business had grown enough to pay significant income tax. Charley had earned a reputation for doing quality work on difficult projects others would not tackle. One project that caught his eye was a lakeside cottage on which the owner wanted to add a second floor and a new roof. It would be a while, though, before the owner could afford the job.

Eighteen months passed. It was spring and Charley had plenty of prospects lined up, but no signed contracts. If just half of his prospects actually materialized, it would be another good year. The last year was busy enough that Charley would owe taxes. Since it was the end of March and he not yet started his tax return, he had to move fast. The paperwork was so backed up that Charley felt he would have to spend the next two weeks working on nothing but taxes to ensure making the April 15 deadline.

The phone messages stacked up as Charley worked exclusively on gathering the documents his accountant needed to complete the tax forms. Among the unanswered messages was the call he wanted most of all--the cottage addition and new roof.

Selling Sin #2

Two intense weeks later. Charley had finally finished his taxes. He frantically began returning the calls. His heart sank. The owner of the cottage, frustrated with not receiving so much as a return call, had given the job to another contractor. You see, the most frustrating feeling a <u>customer</u> can have is to be ready and willing to spend a significant amount of his hard-earned money and not be able to find someone who wants the job.

If Charley wants to stay gainfully self-employed, he must learn to structure his work days so that nothing is left begging for even two days, much less two weeks. To let bookkeeping and taxes take a back seat for 11 and a half months of the year is not a viable way to run a business. No piece of a viable business can be left unattended for two weeks. As Charley illustrates, the unattended piece has a way of having a disproportionate impact on the small business owner. In this case, the tail (taxes) ends up wagging the dog (Charley). All the time and money expended to land the big job was wasted. Now an even longer wait and more effort may be required to land even a small piece of replacement work at the site. Like our youth, the loss from this type of mistake can never be recovered.

A Follow-up System

Timing follow up correctly requires a system for recording and monitoring every prospect you encounter. Begin by asking every prospect you meet for a business card. If they do not have a card, get some written document with the key information about them. Some items I have used include magnetic refrigerator stickers, business receipts with the company name printed on them, a pen or pencil with the company logo, perhaps a label for the company product--if nothing else, at least a piece of scratch paper with the information written by hand.

As you gather these various documents, make notes about what was said at the time. If the prospect asked that you call back in two weeks, make note of it. Names to contact are very important. Sometimes you learn the identity of other decisionmakers. Write that down. As you speak with the prospect, make note of any information that may be useful later in the sales cycle. You may be able to gather more information than will fit on the business card or document you received from the prospect. Keep a notepad handy. It is unprofessional to fumble for paper when the prospect is cooperating in an amicable conversation.

At the end of a work day, it is extremely important to gather the day's harvest of prospect information in a common format. It seems harder to get this job done on days when you happen upon a prospect during the course of other chores than when the day is spent exclusively on marketing--but it must get done. I use old punch cards. They fit nicely in the cover of my appointment book and are large enough for all the information I gather. For those who don't have these computer relics, a set of 3-by-5 note cards will work well.

If you received a business card, glue it to the upper right corner of the record card. Otherwise, write the prospect name and address in that space. Then, enter any pertinent notes you may have acquired from your note pad. The most important task is to create a column for listing the date of your next follow up. If the prospect asked you to call back in two weeks, enter that date. Enter a brief reminder of what was discussed during each call and the deadline for steps you agreed to take. File away in a separate deck those prospects that have grown cold. Update the deck of current prospects and stack it based on the follow-up date.

Barriers and Battlefields

Keep the deck with you all the time. Keep a blank card or two in your car and in your appointment book. On a cold calling day, write your notes directly on the card instead of in your notepad. If you have told a prospect you will get back on a certain date, be sure you do it. If you say you will send some information, do it promptly so that it will be received while your conversation with the prospect is still fresh in his mind.

Follow up works in and of itself. I have personally experienced sales where the prospect's primary reason for buying from me was that I had so professionally followed their need to their window of opportunity. No one else in on the deals even had a chance.

Chapter 24

THE HIDDEN COST OF HIRING

The entrepreneur whose business has grown to the point at which he feels he must hire an employee may think he has made it to the top. Granted, while he is indeed operating on a higher plane, one false step at this point can send a profitable business crashing to the ground. The danger lies in that much of the cost of employees is hidden, and those costs are significant. Workman's Compensation, Unemployment Insurance, and Social Security contributions are quite visible, of course, but the unsuspecting employer can easily encounter double these costs. Three major areas of hidden costs are training, planning, and the natural distance between business owner and employee. Let's look first at the clearly visible costs of adding an employee to a business.

Workman's Compensation

Workman's Compensation is an insurance program designed to cover workers in the event of a major job-related accident. Benefits range from payment of small medical fees to coverage of major medical bills plus a significant portion of an injured employee's wage while he is unable to work.

The cost of this program can be considerable for a small business that has grown to the point of hiring its first part-time employee. The problem is that the minimum premium bears no relation to the length of time an employee may spend on the job. For example, Vera had a wallpapering business that was beginning to keep her busy six days a week, especially during the summer. She thought it would be the perfect time to hire part-time help so she could at least get Saturdays off and not work too late each evening.

Vera talked with her accountant to see what bookkeeping was required. She was surprised to find that she needed insurance. Workman's Compensation required a monthly premium based on a percentage of the hourly wage. Her insurance agent informed her that the premium would be 10 percent of the $7 per hour she intended to pay her helper. It didn't seem like much at first. But as the actual costs became clearer, she realized that the minimum premium would effectively double the rate she had to pay. The problem for small business is that there is a minimum $600 premium and an annual $150 basic processing charge. Her first year expense, therefore, would be at least $750. Therefore:

$$\$7.00 \times 10\% = .70 \text{ divided into } \$750 \text{ minimum premium}, \frac{750}{.70} = 1,070 \text{ hours}$$

1,070 hours represents a half year of part-time help, much more time than Vera had intended to keep the employee. The result is that the effective rate can double or even triple if Vera uses only 333 hours of part-time help.

Vera's business was one that historically had not generated significant Workman's Compensation claims. She was lucky that her monthly percentage was only 10 percent. Other businesses are not so lucky. When Ed went to get Workman's Compensation insurance for his roofing business, his monthly premiums were 100 percent, doubling his hourly pay rate.

Unemployment Compensation

Unemployment Compensation is an insurance plan that spreads the cost of unemployed people across the nation. Again, the basic premium is a percentage of the hourly wage. The difference here is that the percentage is taken only up to the first $7,000 in wages for a given year. The percentage the employer must contribute is based upon industry conditions and the company's individual experience with unemployment claims. A masonry business in a northern state, for example, would have a high rate because of the need to lay off workers every year as cold weather sets in. A company based on stable office jobs would typically face much lower premiums. The starting rate in most industries is 3.5 percent of the hourly wage.

This is an insurance, not a tax. The proceeds are divided, with the state receiving the lion's share of the premiums. The federal government receives .008 percent for the master fund. It is parceled out to states whose own fund has been tapped out due to high unemployment claims. The disbursement of major industrial and agricultural areas throughout the U.S. helps keep the premiums low because there is always one sector up while another may be down.

Social Security Contributions

Our Social Security system requires that employers match employee contributions. The total is currently 15.3 percent of employee gross wages. The employer withholds half--7.65 percent--from the employee's pay. The other half is deposited by the employer along with the employee's withholding. Many small businesses have problems coming up with 15.3 percent for each deposit, plus the federal and state taxes also withheld. The half withheld from the employee often gets lost in small business cash management problems.

Other Employee Costs

Other insurance premiums can actually dictate how you run your business. Dave ran a trucking business and was shocked to find that truck insurance was essentially unobtainable. The premiums were unaffordable if the driver was under age 25. Dave had encountered an insurance Catch-22 situation. He could not find drivers over age 25 for the wages he could afford to pay, and he could not afford to insure the drivers he could afford to hire. He feared that if he charged customers a rate high enough to cover the insurance, his business would be less competitive. This illustrates the problem faced by too many small business owners--their prices do not reflect the total cost of doing business. They unknowingly take risks and only serve to keep the market price artificially low by offering prices that do not turn a profit in the end. Let's look at costs that aren't so black and white.

The Cost of Training

Much more significant, especially at the outset, are costs associated with the entrepreneur coming to grips with the cost of training. Vera quickly learned that cutting a nice straight edge may not be a skill possessed by otherwise competent wallpaper hangers. The process required to lay out corners and holes and miscellaneous angles was another skill she had acquired without realizing the price she had paid to gain it. Vera discovered that training a new employee carried costs in terms of her time that she had not factored in when she decided to hire help. She had to either spend time observing firsthand whether the new employee could paper a tricky corner or be prepared to do the job over herself if the employee couldn't perform the task. A third time-consuming mistake commonly made by unskilled teachers is to constantly look over the shoulder of the new hire, directing every tiny detail of the assigned task. Neither the employee nor the trainer gets much work done and two wages must be deducted from the earnings of one job.

Training a new employee carries costs in two ways. First, it increases the labor cost of any given piece of work. Secondly, it diminishes the effectiveness of the trainer. What Vera could have done as a worker in eight hours, for example, might take her trainee 10 or 12 hours plus two hours of Vera's time. The eight hours of free time Vera had hoped to gain by hiring an employee may total only six hours. When you consider the nonproductive loss of 25 percent of Vera's time, together with the 10 to 12 hours it may take the employee to get the job done, the problem comes into focus. Vera figured she could get a simple job done with $56 in wages ($7 times eight hours). The job actually took the new hire 12 hours plus two hours of Vera's time for training and support. If Vera pays herself $20 per hour, then, the cost of the simple job will be:

$20 x 2 = $40, plus 12 hours x $7.00 = $84 for the helper. Total cost $124

Factor in 3 percent for unemployment, 7.65 percent matching Social Security contribution, and the $700 minimum for workman's compensation and Vera has a genuine cash management problem. Her cost of part-time labor is not the $7 she had expected but more than triple that amount. Vera's time spent with the new hire must diminish quickly. She may decide that the new hire will not cut the mustard and have to start all over again by hiring another employee.

Employee vs. Owner
The most common mistake by entrepreneurs hiring new employees is that they base the hiring considerations upon their own level of skill and personal commitment. The more troublesome of these two considerations is personal commitment. It takes considerable courage, initiative, and responsibility to be self-employed. These characteristics are not shared by the vast majority of employees, particularly when they believe that someone else is in a position to

gain the most from their efforts. The typical new business owner simply assumes that someone they hire will be as committed as themselves. This is never true!

It has been my own experience that when an entrepreneur reaches the stage where they hope to bring in their first manager, they need to factor in a decline of profitability of not less than 30 percent. This is in addition to the increase in wages.

This dramatic drop is due primarily to the different natures of owners and employees. There are many areas where the difference contributes to a decline in profitability. Larry was a builder who also did his own excavating. He had landed a contract to build a home with winter fast approaching. Thanksgiving was just two days away. Ordinarily, it would have been a four day weekend and Larry would have begun the excavation on the following Monday. Late Wednesday afternoon, however, Larry heard the local weather forecast for subzero temperatures beginning Friday night. This meant serious excavation problems because the ground would freeze solid. Zoning authorities would not permit the installation of foundation footings if frost was allowed to set in the ground below. Larry's only opportunity to get the house started before spring was to excavate the basement immediately. That meant working full days on Thanksgiving and the following Friday. He would have to dig the hole and cover it with straw to prevent the entry of frost. When the deep freeze passed, the footings could be poured and the project could get under way before spring.

No employee I know would have come to the rescue of the project by sacrificing his holiday weekend. Operating a small business frequently requires the owner to step up to such crises. Employees can rarely be relied upon to do so. And so it should be. Otherwise, everyone would be a business owner.

Planning Employee Workload

Another major area of unexpected employee cost is planning to keep them busy for a full work day. First, work must be scheduled effectively based upon what a worker can accomplish in a given day. That leads to the logistics of getting in place the materials required for a full day's work. In Larry's case, he had to be sure that all the building materials a crew of workers required to get through a given day were at hand. Availability of materials was only part of the problem. Material had to be in the right place so that time was not wasted moving a whole pile of material to get at bottom pieces. This meant Larry had to schedule the arrival of materials from various vendors and be present when materials were delivered so that what was needed first was in front, not in back or on the bottom.

Larry quickly discovered that planning the workday of only a few employees consumed all his time. He was forced to rely upon the ability of those he had hired to deal expediently with each mini-crisis as it arrived. He also learned that he had to cover the cost of mistakes that were made, including his own. Larry had not planned on the costs generated by employee mistakes. Wages must still be paid for work which must be redone, as well as the second attempt. The balance of increased "payroll costs" comes due when Larry has to pay for materials that must be replaced and to fix equipment broken by misuse.

The Test

A major test along the road to success, then, is whether the entrepreneur can rise to the new challenges that stem from adding employees to a business. The skills required are almost always acquired on the job, in the line of fire. As a practical matter, it is best to significantly overestimate the cost of employees before you decide to take the major growth step that hiring employees represent. Review the "Stair Steps To Success" and "The Node Of Profitability" sections in *"The Small Business Survival Guide"* before you take the plunge. You cannot anticipate every challenge, but you can enhance your ability to deal with these challenges by being better prepared from the beginning.

Chapter 25

THE BATTLE OF IMAGE VS. EGO

Years spent calling upon small businesses have led me to believe that the image one holds of self-employment is the primary reason behind many small business start-ups. But aspiring to project a particular image is not the best strategy when trying to pull off a major undertaking such as gainful self-employment. Certainly, there are instances in which a carefully cultivated image has contributed to making a company great. But the best company image always follows sustained performance rather than precedes it. Herein lies the fatal flaw for start-ups whose motivation is a glorified image of self-employment. It is a mistake to believe that success stems from starting with upscale office space, brand new equipment, classy stationery and a fancy wardrobe. Equally fatal is believing that image can be bought.

Image Problems

Three problem areas with business image are immediately apparent. The first stems from the dreamy fantasy some small business owners have of the image they feel they must project to succeed. Their view too often is disconnected from the reality of what it takes to be successfully self-employed. Then there is the heavy drain upon the small business' cash position that is required to mold an image. Finally, the true nature of image is never really under our control. It is the result of how others perceive you--not how you perceive yourself. The image you actually project is typically far from the one you dream of having. Give this some thought and see if you agree.

Image vs. Reality

Far too many small business ventures are inspired by the image projected by television and movies. We never see a movie about the 60- to 80-hour work weeks that most entrepreneurs struggle to endure. We never get to read an accounting of the billions of dollars annually which have been lost to entrepreneurial risk. We never see the carcasses of hundreds of thousands of failed small businesses strewn across the American business landscape. Instead, we are shown jetsetting millionaires--not hard at work, but in the sound byte moments when they show themselves at glittering parties or sit for media profile interviews.

A case in point is the popular television show *Lifestyles of the Rich and Famous.* At the rate of one grandiose success story per week, there is enough material worldwide to keep the program going for years. If the show profiled only one American a week, we would learn about 52 image makers annually from a pool of 252 million Americans--that represents .00000011, or 11/100,000ths of one percent. The definition of success upon which the program is based represents an incredibly small number of talented, hardworking, and lucky people. Statistically speaking, making it to the level of these image makers is on par with being hit by lightning while holding the winning lottery ticket. You must stay focused on image as the end of a process, not the starting point. So where do we start?

The Starting Line

If one tries to begin with the grandiose and back into a small business plan, the result is a plan that must include assumptions based upon years of prior success. That is the trap. Experience isn't a given for a new entrepreneur. Those people of image, who have achieved great success, have done so in part due to factors which have permitted them to begin not at the starting line, but well ahead of it. Consider these factors that permit a head start.

Self-confidence is extremely important to a small business. Has the confidence level of the entrepreneur been nurtured from childhood or is it only developing under the demands of entrepreneurship? Has there been early learning and direction by association that may provide an early lead? Is a quality, hard-earned, debt-free college education part of the package the entrepreneur brings to the table, or is general education growing right along with business education? Did the entrepreneur arrive with a solid work ethic, or was a work ethic forced upon him by contractual commitments and the prospect of bankruptcy? Was there access to capital outside the constraints of commercial finance?

Timeliness is also important. Lady Luck has visited many image makers. If not in the form of a winning lottery ticket, perhaps in the guise of a timely job opening...owning a few shares of stock at just the right time...or a blip in the marketplace at precisely the right moment. Unfortunately, the vast majority of small businesses owners do not begin with so much going for them. They leave from the starting line or perhaps behind it.

Image is Earned, not Bought

Whatever our starting point, we will do well to remember that we develop an image rather than buy one. We prepare ourselves for success with daily contributions to our ability to capitalize upon opportunity when it arrives. Experience has shown me that we need to do only one thing just right, at the right time in our 35-year working life, to become an image maker. The problem: most entrepreneurs are not ready when opportunity knocks. So when the door swings open, it smacks them in the face. One small success stacked upon another contributes to our ability to build an image that is real and may not cost a dime. "Jimmy always gets the job done on time." "Peter's work is always worth what he charges." "Joan's work is always finished within the budget." The further we go, and the more we accomplish, the more we are recognized as having that special something that separates us from the crowd.

Joan's image precedes her as those around her spread the word that she always finishes under budget. The circle of recognition advances like the ripples of a pebble thrown into a pond. The image Joan projects is based on the reality that she delivers the goods. The goal of living the lifestyle we see in the movies becomes unavailable for Joan if she instead sets out to attain it through the clothes she wears, an upscale business address, and an office full of new equipment. Even the most unsophisticated employee can judge whether work is done on time and costs more than it should. Joan instead achieves her image when day-to-day accomplishment draws the envy and praise of others. Customers want her to handle their accounts. Employees want to work for her. When her recognition reaches the outside, already successful people want her to become part of their fraternity. Soon, the investment community rallies to the smell of success and Joan is on her way.

The Cost of Image Building

The Small Business Survival Guide outlines the concept of The Entrepreneurial Trojan Horse. This is when beliefs held by owners and employees destroy a business from within. The problem illustrates the need sometimes to play down success in an effort to conserve cash. Image building is the antithesis of the Entrepreneurial Trojan Horse. It seeks to plant into the minds of onlookers, and even those within the company, the belief that things are going very well. Typically this is evidenced by financial flamboyance--tailored suits, fancy company cars and luxury hideaways.

Employees react to the success they see around them whether it is real or merely projected to create an image. They will demand higher pay and more benefits. They will encourage spending for better equipment and finer facilities. If employees believe they are not getting their share of the perks, they can work against the company in ways too subtle for the busy executive to recognize. The company picnic and Christmas party take on new, highly-political dimensions. The sales force is no longer satisfied with meeting in the company conference room--they want all-expense paid trips to luxury weekend resorts. Then there are the club memberships for upper level management and an occasional company meeting. None of these amenities can be provided on a low-cost budget because image building requires the best of everything.

When we translate all these considerations into the cost of image building, even large businesses run out of money. Jason's company was doing business in a dozen states and appeared to be capable of growing dramatically. When Jason wanted to build an image, he turned to several public relations firms that specialized in developing national business images. The theory was that a company with a nationally recognized name could easily land clients across the country. Jason headed to the public relations capitol--New York City. Several trips were necessary, of course, so that Jason's management team could meet with PR executives to map a strategy that would project the desired image. Their collective ideas reflected the breadth and scope of what was "possible" in the world of image building.

Jason particularly liked the idea of developing a new index similar to the Dow Jones Industrial Average we hear daily. Jason's business was in touch with more than 20,000 small businesses on a daily basis through his franchisees. He felt certain that a small business index, especially one that bore his company name, would provide just the leverage he needed to take his business, and himself, into the limelight. The PR consultants staged a media blitz for Jason in New York City that made Jason feel really important.

Seeking Approval

At the heart of the desire to build an image is the need for approval on a very high level. This seldom has anything to do with sound business practice. Question the executives of image-conscious companies and they will have very elaborate positions on why image is so necessary--why no expense can be spared to be recognized on a very high scale. The problem is that only one in 100,000 of these executives has ever built an image with his own money and with his own company on the line.

On his media blitz, Jason was treated like a genuine millionaire, something that didn't happen back home because everyone in the company knew he was "just plain folks" who struggled for what he had. But in New York, he appeared at last to be getting the recognition he had sought all along. The PR consultants arranged limousine transportation from the airport to one important place after another. They had arranged introductions to a stream of high-ranking New York executives. There was not a free moment in his schedule. Jason felt he had been accepted into the fraternity of big-business national entrepreneurs. In the process, he became addicted to the glamour. He became obligated by his desire to maintain this new, exciting lifestyle to proceed with the image-building process for the company.

To the people around Jason, it was apparent that he had been caught up in the jetsetting lifestyle. There were television commercials and more whirlwind trips to New York, but no stock index bearing his company name. The commercials generated inquiries at a cost of something like $5,000 each--nearly three years of revenue from a single new client. The PR people had done an outstanding job in only one respect--Jason owed them some very big fees and commissions. The PR people had pumped up Jason long enough for the image industry to extract the heart and sole from his growing business. In two years he was broke. His once thriving business was taken over for the amount of its debt. Jason was left with nothing.

Jason failed to understand the true source of image. He gambled that image can be built with advertsiement and promotion. Occasionally it happens. But at what price? The process that had made him successful in the beginning--building upon one small success at a time, was abandoned in favor of a single, all-or-nothing roll of the dice. He bet all his years of hard work on creating the image of overnight success and lost it all.

Chapter 26

THE ENTREPRENEURIAL MIRAGE

If one could take to the streets and peer past the storefronts and into the depths of small business operations, all too often one would find an empty shell. There are several window dressings commonly used by entrepreneurs to create the image that they are running a business, when in fact, they are not. It is relatively easy to discern the difference between an operation that is a real business and one which is nothing more than a hopeful activity. The difference lies in whether the operator accepts the social responsibility that comes with operating a business. Without meeting these obligations, a business person is simply carrying out the functions of a technician. Is the mechanic running a repair business or is he simply repairing cars? Is the beauty operator running a salon or simply styling hair?

A business that does not treat employees as an asset, and does not pay its fair share toward fundamental benefit programs, is not a true business. Even less honorable are operators who believe they can hide questionable behavior. They delude themselves even further when they think that getting away with shady practices for a couple of years means they are home free.

The first test is how the entrepreneur deals with his employees. Does the company accounting system show the proper taxes withheld? Are workman's compensation premiums being paid? Is unemployment insurance being paid for all wages earned? And are withheld taxes being deposited on time in the name of the employee? I have frequently seen "entrepreneurs" search frantically for a way to avoid their fair share of these necessary insurance programs and the taxes we must contribute.

"I don't have any employees," Chuck argues. "Almost all the guys on this job are subcontractors. Those two guys over there are just day labor. I pay them cash at the end of the day." By declaring his workers subcontractors and day wage earners, Chuck is adopting a position in which he believes he is not liable for workman's compensation premiums, unemployment compensation premiums, matching social security taxes and the accounting necessary to file all the associated taxes. Ironically, most of the small business owners who adopt this strategy never reap the benefits they believe they can achieve by shortchanging the system. There is nothing left over because the price Chuck negotiated for his job was too low. It did not provide for mandatory benefits and tax compliance. When he is caught, he will not have the resources to pay his debt to the system and Chuck will lose his business.

He has put his operation at substantial risk believing that he has outfoxed the revenuers. Chuck doesn't realize that the revenuers have heard all this nonsense before. Here is a crucial business definition from Publication 334, *Tax Guide For Small Business,* published by the IRS and provided free to entrepreneurs.

> ***Common-law employees:*** *Where common law rules, every individual who performs services subject to the will and control of the employer, as to both what must be done and how it must be done, is an employee. It does not matter that the employer allows the employee discretion and freedom of action, so long as the employer has the legal right to control both the method and the result of the services.*

Two usual characteristics of an employee-employer relationship are that the employer has the right to discharge the employee and the employer supplies tools and a place to work.

If you have an employer-employee relationship, it makes no difference how it is described. It does not matter if the employee is called an employee, partner, co-adventurer, agent, or independent contractor. It does not matter how the payments are made, or what they are called. Nor does it matter whether the individual is employed full time or part time.

Chuck has a big problem with the IRS. Every worker Chuck is calling something other than an employee is really an employee. The penalty will cost Chuck the taxes that should have been withheld but were not, plus an amount equal to that for not making the withholding.

But the IRS is only part of the problem. State and local taxing bodies take their share as well. Then there are the claims if someone is injured on the job or if a disgruntled worker files for unemployment. Attorneys have a field day with entrepreneurs like Chuck when there is an injury. If he is worth a dime, they will come after him in court and make him look very much like a crook. The costs of the legal battle and health care for the injury will surely mount faster than Chuck's cash position can cover. The first mirage, then, is believing you are in business if you are not dealing with employee taxes and mandatory benefits. Employees do not deal with these problems, but business owners do!

The Sweet Little Cash Business

As a young salesman, I recall riding through the streets of Chicago talking with a fellow employee about one day owning our own business. "One of these days I'm going to start me up one of those little hot dog stands like that one on the corner over there," Mike said. "It's a great little cash business." Mike was alluding to his belief that since the sales were all cash and no paperwork was required, one would be able to siphon off money without paying the taxes due, thereby enhancing the take of his little enterprise.

Like the business person who denies the existence of employees, an operator with this outlook is fooling himself. Every business is part of a bigger picture. There is no such beast as a sweet little cash business that leaves no paper trail. Two possible exceptions might be gun running and drug smuggling, both of which present more threatening liabilities than taxes. Every business has vendors that supply material, customers who frequent the establishment, and employees who run the place. If the IRS gets suspicious, even a rookie auditor can recreate your spending records in a flash. A couple short interviews with employees, or two days on site when deliveries are being made, can provide a list of suppliers with whom you have done business. For example, Sam the auditor is present when the hot-dog bun delivery truck arrives. Sam casually asks the driver how many buns he usually delivers and what is the largest order that Mike's business has placed. Sam could also go directly to the office of that vendor and obtain vendor records. I have been present at two such visits, and can assure you that vendors eagerly supply a full record at the mere sight of an IRS identification card.

The IRS computer database is a library of business tax filings for every conceivable line of work. The computer creates a Standard Industrial Classification (SIC) code profile of the type of business Mike is running, complete with typical percentages for each of the expenses associated with that type of business by geographical area. (The ZIP code is part of the tax form.) Once the auditor has a single piece of simple information, such as how many hot-dog buns have been purchased, he can simply reverse the math. He uses the percentages from the computer profile to compute typical industry operating costs and project what gross sales must have been to have required that quantity of hot-dog buns. If your sales are in line, the audit is short and relatively easy. If your figures are out of line, get ready for a much more penetrating look.

It's Only a Matter of Time

Successfully cutting corners for a time carries no guarantee that you are getting away with anything. The IRS is not the all-knowing, all-seeing deity they are typically made out to be. It may be years before they ever get wind of an abuse. But you are never safe from having to finally pay the price. Brett ran a cash business from vending machines right up until his untimely death. He had as many as 30 employees bringing in as much as $30,000 a day in vending machine receipts. Brett had fooled himself into thinking that he could run such an empire without keeping records, even for his checking account. He believed that if there is cash in the bank account, everything is OK. And it was until a blip came along. The stress from knowing that no income taxes were being withheld and no sales tax was being deposited was apparently more than he could handle. He died young of a massive heart attack.

Ownership of the company changed hands to Brett's wife, Jane. Even though she had been married to Brett for many years, she knew very little about the business. It was only days before she reported tax figures that didn't jibe with any previous records and the floodgates opened. Every taxing body ever associated with the business pulled an audit. What the family thought was to have been a large inheritance turned out to be one can of worms after another. Back taxes came to six figures. The bank account was discovered to contain a $150,000 floating overdraft. That is, the account was overdrawn by $150,000, but daily deposits of cash from the vending machines for years had been sufficient to cover the checks that would be cleared each day.

What had been a multi-million dollar business is down to two employees with $3,000 a day in cash receipts. Tax collectors and other vendors line up for weekly cash payments as they no longer accept checks from the business. Brett's son, who runs what is left of the business, would have been much better off to start from scratch than to hang around and clean up the pieces. He has already spent two years backpedaling and it may take two more before matters are settled. But Brett has learned to be in business and not simply run a vending machine route. He will do things right and leave his children more than an empty vessel of an estate.

Sooner or Later, You Must Pay the Piper

This brings us to a final point--paying a fair share. Those of us fortunate enough to accumulate some wealth, do so by reducing our annual tax burden through business write-offs. If these write-offs were not permitted, then in each tax year our tax burden would grow, sometimes much larger. As entrepreneurs, we are permitted to roll our earnings into a larger and larger equity ball which is essentially funded by postponement of tax payments. This equity is not cash, but it is ours to convert to cash whenever we choose. So many entrepreneurs I have known somehow lose track of how it was that they were able to create a large, untaxed equity ball.

Somehow they forget the benefits they have received from the tax money of others. Customers came to their door on paved roads--kept clean in the summer, plowed in the winter, and repaired to last for many years. It was the local police that kept the business from being burglarized and the local fire department that was ready to save their business in event of a fire. The school system educated their children and others. It may have been this education that taught people how to use the entrepreneur's high-tech product. And it was our national government, as slow and inefficient as it sometimes seems, that has created a free economic zone that has allowed small business to flourish as nowhere else on earth.

It must be remembered that much of entrepreneurial gain comes from tax laws that permit risk takers to push forward an ever larger untaxed gain. Employees whose income is totally documented as taxable income each year have no such privilege. To take it all as we build our empire and not be willing to pay the piper in the end smacks of compulsive greed. Granted, we need not spend a dime more than tax law requires. Neither should we come to the end of our entrepreneurial journey and commit fraud to hide profits and avoid taxes on income that the system has made possible. Auditors know that the only people who do not pay tax are those who have not earned enough to owe tax. Pay the tax bill with a smile on your face and the knowledge that you are among the few, the entrepreneurs, who helped make the system what it is. You see, the true mark of a successful entrepreneur is having won the opportunity to pay a whopping tax bill.

CONCLUSION

My firm belief is that entrepreneurship is a wonderful way to journey through life. So much so that I have already spent a significant part of my journey illuminating the entrepreneurial path for those who follow me. Regardless of the individual's definition of success--great riches, abundant leisure, recognition, freedom--we all encounter problems from the same pool of human experience. Being a business owner, however, magnifies the variety of the human experience beyond that of individuals who never venture beyond the family and nine-to-five job.

The constant barrage of new employees, new ideas, new vendors, new customers, new competition and so on, exposes us to an endless procession of different personalities. They come from various backgrounds and bring with them a world of diverse experiences from which they make the decisions that take them through each day. To their input, we add our own bias and experience, good and bad, hoping to end that day by having gained on our position of the previous day. The process is remarkable and complex when we stop to think about it.

For me, new observations have surfaced as these thoughts have been captured on the page. Among them is that the difference between a success story and a complete failure is some very small margin of a commodity. Sometimes the commodity is luck. I have known business owners who have succeeded despite themselves. Perhaps it is coincidence. Some thriving entrepreneurs cannot explain how they succeeded. They were simply in the right place at the right time. Occasionally, small business success hinges on the ability to stick with a problem for one more step than the competition. I have witnessed numerous small business success stories where the difference was a single, seemingly insignificant, additional effort. Sometimes the resulting victory over failure is a solution that came from genius, other times it is by simple accident. The Wright brothers succeeded by improving on the principles of flight. Fleischmann and Ponds may have created fusion in a beaker by accident--and so it goes.

Small business ownership has established a horrible record of trampling the hopes and dreams of one entrepreneur after another. Only one in five makes it past the fifth year in operation. Of the survivors, few can claim a lifetime of successful self employment. Rarer still are those who manage successful self employment and a healthy family life. I am convinced that it doesn't have to be that way. When an entrepreneur encounters a new barrier or battlefield, he--more than any of his brothers and sisters--is better equipped to deal with it and move beyond.

Barriers and Battlefields by definition focuses upon the problems encountered in running a small business. My purpose is not to discourage the entrepreneur, but to expose him to problems before they are encountered. It is also to help those who have already encountered these problems and have found themselves floundering in search of solutions. I have illustrated these problems at the risk of painting a picture to which some may respond with resignation.

I use this technique without reservation, as I know that a true entrepreneur is not thwarted by exposure to layers of problems. He instead is strengthened by his expanding vision. The typical entrepreneur consistently shows the ability to recognize and therefore deal with problems. This is the weapon with which he sets those problems aside and moves on. *Barriers and Battlefields* is an effort to expose the entrepreneur to problems he has yet to recognize because they have worn a convincing disguise.

Every entrepreneur has been exposed to the very problems documented in this book, but only a few could discern their true source. I speak from experience.

Once you have become aware of the real barriers facing your entrepreneurial venture, you will gain new resolve and direction with which you can push your quest to the next level. It has certainly done that for me and for *No Entry Accounting*.

If these pages serve only to put you in touch with enough new understanding to do the things that small business owners need to do, then this work is a success. It doesn't have to be a total change. Perhaps you will listen more closely to a bit of advice. Maybe you will seek to work more effectively with a difficult, but talented employee. Perhaps you will have recognized some shortcoming of your own that has kept you from success.

Remember, the difference between success and failure is very small indeed. The high failure rate of small business doesn't have to be that way. Balance is the key to having it all. Accept new input. Reason more amicably. Work to solve problems rather than waste time assigning blame. Share your entrepreneurial advantage and get more back than a successful business. Successful entrepreneurship does indeed comprise the American dream.

Index

Accounting
    accrual 50
    cash 50
    paradox 49
    perception 5
Addiction
    codependency 96-97
    process 80, 88- 89
    shifting 82
    substance 80-81
Advertising
    word of mouth 156
    increasing 157
Alcoholism 82
    blackouts 84
    cost 86
    customers 86
    employees 85
    liability 85
    recognizing 87
Cash
    management 71
    proceeds 20
    saving 74
Collateral
    customers 19
    developing 18
Computers
    documentation 27
    expedience 29
    misconceptions 28
    platform 32
    processor 34
    RAM 34
    scope 26
    speed 32
    storage 35
    threshold 29, 31, 35
    training 30
DCA
    business 100, 103
    community 104
    defined 99
    history 101-102
Decisions
    perfectionism 111
    workaholism 110
    control 113
Downtime 72
Equity
    borrowed 20
    customers 19
    home 18
Hiring
    cost 170-171
    FICA 171
    profitability 172
    training 171
    unemployment compensation 170
    workload 173
    workman's compensation 169
Image 175
    created 177
    cost 178
    fallacy 176, 181-183
    trap 179
Income
    created 18-20
    psychic 21
Legal
    proceedings 137
    research 139
    risk management 142-145
    small claims 138
    suit 140
Logic
    commitment 124
    signs 123
Marketing
    spinoffs 8
    testing 6
Money
    success 14
    management 43-47
No Entry Accounting ™ 4, 9, 79, 103, 151
    box 5-6
    testing 5, 7
Perfectionism *(see Process Addiction)*
Portfolio
    assembly 160-161
    materials 162

       organizing 160
       presentation 161
Pricing 115
       discount 122
       excessive 118
       hourly 116-117
       logic 121
       policies 57
       setting 60
       volumes 59
Prime
       curve 13
       forecast 16
       recovery 13
       startup 15
Printers 37
       limitations 38-39
       size 38, 40
       types 39
Process Addiction 80
       behavior 88, 91
       facing 96
       perfectionism 95, 111
       recognizing 89
       secrecy 95
       triangulation 93
       trust 94
       workaholism 92, 94
Proceeds 20
Profit 15
Quick Cash Report 51-52
Records
       audit 148
       IRS 147
       storing 148-150
Research 3
Sales
       followup 164
       mistakes 165-166
       persistence 164
       system 167
       timeliness 163
Sexuality
       abuse 128
       counseling 133
       genetic 127
       power 132
       workplace 130

Small Business Survival Guide 21, 79, 174
Small Business Total
   Information System 9-10, 55
Taxes
       FICA 69
       Form 2210 65
       managing 63, 183
       projecting 64
Testing 5-7
Workaholism *(see Process Addiction)*

Ordering Information

The *No Entry Accounting*™ materials, *The Small Business Total Information System,* and *The Small Business Survival Guide* are available directly from No Entry Accounting. For information, write or call:

>   No Entry Accounting
>   36W794 Stonebridge Lane
>   St. Charles, IL 60175
>   (708) 584-7426

The Small Business Survival Guide is available in hardcover for $29.95 postage paid within the United States and Canada. Illinois residents add sales tax.

The *No Entry Accounting*™ materials are available for $39.95 within three weeks of receipt of the prepaid order. For rush processing add $6. Illinois residents add sales tax.

The Small Business Total Information System includes *The Small Business Survival Guide,* the *No Entry Accounting*™ materials, a complete set of system programs, and a reference manual. The system includes some 170 programs and more than 60 reports providing the most comprehensive small business system available. The heart of the system is No Entry Accounting. The programs run in a Windows environment as Excel spread sheets. The minimum configuration is a 386/20, 4MB RAM, 40MB hard drive and a printer. Job cost users would likely want to add 2 to 4 MB of RAM for performance enhancement. The package runs well on any 486. An informative brochure is available. The package price is $249, postage paid in the U.S. and Canada. Illinois residents add sales tax.

A packaged system including hardware, all software, and two days on-site training is available. Nearly all users become fully operational with two days of training. Call for your nearest licensed *No Entry Accounting*™ dealer. Dealerships are also available.

VISA and MasterCard are accepted.